ENDORSEMENTS

"Dr. Dean skillfully humanizes the savagery and confusion of America's 'Forgotten War' through the words and senses of young Roy Blanchard."

—Dr. Michael Passineau, Professor of Medicine, Drexel University College of Medicine

"Dr. Dean tells, for the first time, the story of Roy Blanchard, and offers us a valuable history of what it was like to fight in the trenches of WWI as a doughboy. This type of first-hand account is welcomed, indeed."

—Dr. Jeff Johnson, Associate Professor at Providence College and author of *They Are All Red Out Here: Socialist Politics in the Pacific Northwest, 1895–1925*

"A fascinating piece of military history, brought to you through the experiences of young Roy Blanchard. Roy was an exceptional young man that volunteered to fight in America's 'Forgotten War.' We owe our freedom to men like Roy. Read this book!"

—Kevin J. Mather, President and COO, Seattle Mariners Baseball Club

★ ★ ★ ★ ★

COURAGE

ROY BLANCHARD'S JOURNEY IN AMERICA'S FORGOTTEN WAR

PAUL DEAN

LUCIDBOOKS

Courage
Copyright © 2016 by Paul Dean

Published by Lucid Books in Houston, TX.
www.LucidBooks.net

First Printing 2016

ISBN-10: 1-63296-096-6
ISBN-13: 9781632960962
eISBN-10: 1-63296-097-4
eISBN-13: 9781632960979

Page xi, 1, 65, 183, and 184—Photos of Roy Blanchard and his family are used with permission of the Blanchard family.

Page 84—German Soldiers at a camouflaged Howitzer during World War I. 1914-15. Artillery was the major weapon of WWI, accounting for 60% of casualties. Everett Historical/Shutterstock.com

Page 89—Yanks Going into Action France - Early 1900 postcard depicting Yankee soldiers going into action in France during WWI. Susan Law Cain/ Shutterstock.com

Page 117—American pilots and mechanics prepare for daylight raids on German trenches and cities. Petite Sythe, France. WWI. Aug. 16, 1918. Everett Historical/Shutterstock.com

Page 166—American troops ride on WWI tanks going forward to the battle line in the Forest of Argonne, France. Sept. 26, 1918. Everett Historical/ Shutterstock.com

Cover image: World War One Soldiers Silhouettes Below Cloudy Skyline At Dusk or Dawn. PANGI/Shutterstock.com

Special Sales: Most Lucid Books titles are available in special quantity discounts. Custom imprinting or excerpting can also be done to fit special needs. Contact Lucid Books at info@lucidbooks.net.

CONTENTS

Their story is known to all of you. It is the story of the American man at arms...From one end of the world to the other, he has drained deep the chalice of courage. As I listened to those songs of the glee club, in memory's eye I could see those staggering columns of the First World War, bending under soggy packs on many a weary march, from dripping dusk to drizzling dawn, slogging ankle deep through mire of shell-pocked roads; to form grimly for the attack, blue-lipped, covered with sludge and mud, chilled by the wind and rain, driving home to their objective, and for many, to the judgment seat of God.

—General Douglas MacArthur,
Farewell Speech, May 1962

DEDICATION

EW SOLDIERS TELL their stories. The memories are too painful, they don't think they are heroes (the ones who didn't make it back are the heroes), or they don't think civilians will understand.

This is the story of a young man from the American Midwest who, in autumn of 1918, found himself in France on the front lines of World War I. Corporal Roy Blanchard was one of thousands of Yanks in the US Army's 32nd Division who had their feet on the fire step, awaiting the whistle that would call them to climb over the top of the trench into a muddy, barbed wire, and corpse-filled No Man's Land. If they could survive the machine guns, artillery, and sniper fire, they would storm the opposing trenches and force the Germans backward. If they could win enough of these battles, they would force the German bully out of France and end this long, senseless war.

Most people know that the US was on the winning side of World War I. Yet, most people do not know what it was like. The submarine-infested Atlantic Ocean, the muddy stalemate of the Western Front, the horror of No Man's Land, and the wonder of squadrons of airships flying overhead at over 100 mph all were new and terrible innovations of the war. Young men had to live in the muddy world of trenches, endure hours of shelling, and repeatedly summon the courage to go over the top. Roy's experiences in the US and France show us what it was like to leave home, go through hell on earth, and come home and try to make sense of it all.

In many ways, Roy's story didn't have much chance of being told. When I was working on my master's thesis at Washington State University, I found myself captivated by President Wilson's speeches justifying US entry into World War I. I wondered whether the soldiers who fought in the war believed they were fighting for the reasons that Wilson articulated so eloquently: "To live and be at ease from organized wrong," and "To make the world safe for democracy," or perhaps for their own reasons. Remembering back to college conversations, I asked my former college unit-mate Michael Passineau if his grandfather who fought in the First World War had kept a diary. Sure enough, he had. Mike's mother, Ruth, agreed to send me her father's diary, but on her way to send the package, she stopped by for coffee with her old friend Amy Blanchard Bowden. Over coffee, Amy asked Ruth what she was up to, and Ruth replied that she was sending her father's World War I diary to a friend of her son.

Amy remarked, "That's interesting; my grandfather served in World War I as well."

It's Amy's grandfather, Roy Blanchard, who is the subject of this work. Roy was told by his commanding officers not to keep a diary, but since he believed his time in France was going to be the most remarkable event in his life, he kept one anyway. He also wrote letters to his mother, brother, and his sister Pearl. Thankfully, Pearl kept those letters. The last piece for my research was finding the story of Roy's regiment, the 126th, which was written in 1920 and published by the 126th Association in Grand Rapids, Michigan. There it languished in obscurity (at least as far as I was concerned) until a few years back when I discovered the book on one of my internet searches for all things World War I. Finding this book meant that all of the events Roy had made mention of, I could now discover the broader context and finish this story.

Roy was one of the millions of young men who volunteered or was selected by the government to fight for the US in the most brutal war in the history of mankind up to that point. This work is dedicated to all the unsung soldiers who have summoned the courage to go *over the top*. Your story deserves to be told.

I dedicate this book to the Blanchard family, who shared their memories of a truly unsung hero, especially Amy Blanchard Bowden, who offered to send her grandfather's priceless letters to a total stranger, and Clark Blanchard, who talked openly about his father and who reminds many of Roy.

And finally to Kathryn, Nathan, Carolyn, Alaina, and Lizzie who all inspire me in various ways and have all sacrificed to make completing this work possible.

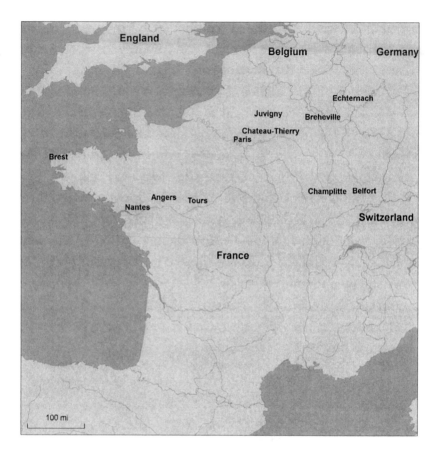

Key locations for Roy Blanchard and the 126th Infantry Regiment in France. They landed in Brest, saw their first action on the Western Front outside Belfort, and took part in major advances near Chateau-Thierry. Roy and the 126th were outside of Breheville when the war ended. The 126th occupied the Germany city of Echternach in 1919.

PREFACE

Roy Blanchard Guarding the Texas Border, 1916

———— ★ ★ ★ ★ ★ ————

WITHIN THE RANKS of khaki-clad American soldiers was nineteen-year-old Roy Blanchard. Smartly, he marched away from Paris and toward German lines on a narrow road, in line with nearly 4,700 fellow soldiers of the 126th infantry regiment. Four men made up a row, twenty-five rows of men made up a platoon, and one-hundred yards separated each platoon. Most of these men were teenagers like Roy, drawn from the American Midwest

They marched in unison, singing from the small song books Uncle Sam had issued to US Soldiers to keep their minds off the long marches. Had any listeners been around, they'd have heard patriotic ballads, familiar hymns, and popular songs like "It's a Long Way to Tipperary." As the road led them into a small forest, they could hear the *krump, krump* of artillery and the faint *rat-a-tat-tat* of machine gun fire in the distance. They switched to single file, adding the steady *crunch, crunch, crunch* of their boots on the gravel path. Their singing stopped.

Distant flares and artillery flashes cast eerie shadows through the trees as they marched out of the forest and into a cool, moonless night. On the eastern outskirts of a small village, French guides joined the Americans and led Roy's 126th quietly into the front lines through the maze of support trenches and barbed-wire entanglements.

Following the French guides, the American soldiers stumbled and ran into each other, making slow progress in the dark. Finally, they arrived at their positions just before 4:00 a.m. Most of the 126th, including Roy's Company K, took positions in reserve trenches a few hundred yards behind the front lines. One group,

Company I, took their spot in a half-mile section of trench on the front lines. The seven-foot-wide, seven-foot-deep trenches had duck-board walks and ran parallel to the German lines, except for the zigzagging communication trenches that ran out into No Man's Land toward the German positions.

Roy, together with his buddies of Company K, entered and took his position. He stepped up onto the fire step, eyes wide open, peering over the parapet and looking toward the Germans hundreds of yards away in the dark. All was quiet save the shuffling of men in wool uniforms and the whispers back and forth. Dawn came slowly for these young men, thousands of miles from home and away from all that was familiar. In the darkness, they thought back to friends and family, who were all back home safe and secure.

All eyes went up as German triplanes buzzed over their lines. In an ineffective response, the French fired anti-aircraft guns at the triplane scouts. Next, they heard the distant *krump, krump* of artillery open up in the distance. Moments passed, and as the shells screamed down toward their position, Roy and his fellow soldiers ducked, making themselves as small a target as possible. The shells' deafening explosions sent showers of dirt and shrapnel in the air together with the *crack* of sharpshooters and *rat-a-tat-tat* of machine-gun fire.

Roy's comrade, Private Joseph W. Guyton of Company I, peeked over the parapet to return fire. But just as he raised his head into view, one bullet from a German machine gun barrage struck him in the forehead, jerking his head back and killing him instantly. The surrounding soldiers stopped and stared at Guyton's body. A moment ago, he had been talking and laughing, and now he was dead. The 126th had prepared for casualties, but the reality of Guyton's immediate death—the first casualty for the 126th regiment on the Western Front—still shocked his teenage comrades.

But the Germans continued to fire their machine guns and load their artillery, so Roy crouched low beneath the parapet and gripped his rifle tightly. Strangely enough his first emotion was anger, not fear.

CHAPTER 1

★ ★ ★ ★ ★

BEGINNINGS

Think of the future, and forget the past.
—ROY TO PEARL, 1918

From Left to Right: John, Roy, Pearl, Lena, and
Earl Blanchard, Circa 1903.

★ ★ ★ ★ ★

SOME PEOPLE START off life with wounds so deep they can only limp through life. Many repeat the abuse or abandonment they suffered as a child. Still, others find the courage to overcome and become the cornerstone that others can build on.

Roy was the first son of John and Lena Blanchard.[1] He was born in Claremont, New Hampshire's largest town in 1908, with a population of 30,000 and every metropolitan advantage except for a city destination.[2] But blue-collar mill jobs and pleasant, wide avenues didn't appeal to John Blanchard, and he soon brought the family west to a farm in Michigan. One family didn't appeal to John Blanchard either. When Roy was in the eighth grade, a policeman knocked on his door and presented Lena evidence that her husband was married to another woman in a town a few miles away. Bigamy was against the law, and the court required John to choose between the two families. While the court did require a choice, it did not require John to inform his family of the reasons why. For Roy, there were no goodbyes, no reasons why. All John left him was a deep and lasting fear of being abandoned. Roy questioned whether he was to blame for his dad leaving. He questioned whether or not he mattered at all. All he knew for sure was that life had dramatically changed and the weight of caring for his family now partially rested on his shoulders. And he didn't have any grand ideas.

Though his mother became a washwoman to earn money, she couldn't care for Roy's younger siblings and pay all the bills. As the

---

1. Roy Blanchard, State of Michigan Marriage License, Kent County Michigan, October 16, 1923.
2. *The Granite Monthly* Vol XL Nos. 4 and 5, April and May 1908.

Michigan cold increased and the money dwindled, Roy dropped out of school and went to the rail yards and taunted the workers from afar. The names, varying between annoying and maddening, continued until they threw coal at him to drive him away. Roy packed up as much coal as he could carry and returned home. As times grew more difficult, his mother, sister, and little brother increasingly relied on him to bring home more than baseball-sized lumps of coal. He chose the best chance for work he had. Throughout his childhood, Roy had watched his father painting buggies, and he acquired some skill secondhand. He tried his hand at painting signs for storefronts: "Apples on sale today."[3] This work and other odd jobs provided enough resources for a time.

Roy's America accepted child labor. The US Census of 1900 showed that 700,000 non-agriculture workers were between ten and fifteen years old. Some worked to support their families while others counted on it to survive. Teenagers worked late at night in New York City as uniformed messengers, newsboys, or bootblacks. Laws passed to protect these vulnerable children and youth were unenforced and ineffective. While Roy did odd jobs in Michigan, New York newsboys brawled over valuable turf, and boys and girls rolled cigars across the Midwest and East Coast. Pennsylvania's youth perhaps braved the most dangerous job. While breathing coal dust for ten hours a day, the young men picked out foreign objects from moving expanses of newly broken coal. Reaching out for the objects, some boys fell in the rushing lines of coal and did not survive. Spending their days in textile mills, coal mines, or city streets, the youth did not have time for reading, writing, and arithmetic; and like Roy, they often didn't finish high school.

Child labor, among other pressing issues, troubled the reformers.

---

3. Clark Blanchard, Roy's first child, interview by author, August 4, 2000.

In order to save children who desperately needed an education, the reformers determined to educate the general public via the newly popular news source—the newspaper. Beginning in 1866, chemists discovered how to make white paper out of chemically digested wood pulp. Wood-pulp paper, far cheaper and more available than waste-rags paper, enabled daily newspapers to expand in the 1880s. Cheap paper, plus the recent streamlining of the process of photo-engraving, gave daily papers new life and appeal. Men like Joseph Pulitzer and William Randolph Hearst took the inexpensive paper and innovative photography, added outsize type, magazine-style Sunday supplements, comics, and sports sections. The public responded by buying more papers that featured investigative reports accelerating progress toward eliminating child labor.

Beyond the effective (if occasionally irresponsible[4]) press, politicians also influenced and were influenced by the patterns of the day. The frustrations of the working man created great unrest in American society while Roy was finding his way. Small businesses, farm, and labor movements had grown tired of feeling helpless in economic matters and asked their government to put aside the traditional doctrines of *laissez-faire* and work directly on their behalf. Roy's challenges, in many ways, typified the age. Adept politicians stepped up and led efforts to regulate industry in order to give men like Roy a better chance to compete and find

---

4. Promoting a conflict with Spain (the conflict that became the Spanish-American War) was the greatest example of irresponsible journalism in this time period. Pulitzer confessed that he liked the idea of a small war that increased circulation. Hearst sent Richard Harding Davis, the most renowned reporter of the day, and Frederic Remington, depicter of the cowboy west, to keep propaganda coming (Hearst told Remington, "You furnish the pictures and I'll furnish the war.") Davis fabricated or exaggerated stories, and Remington furnished the pictures. The overheated American public only needed a spark, which was provided by the sinking of the Maine.

work. Railroads and large firms were the first to face legislative scrutiny. Both Democrats and Republicans vied for the progressive voters, but no election had greater appeal or personality than the election of 1912. This unprecedented three-way race featured a former, current, and future president of the United States. Each candidate, with his own story and approach, strove to improve the conditions that made life difficult for young men like Roy. This election captured Roy's attention, particularly the attempt by charismatic, pugnacious, and courageous Teddy Roosevelt to overcome all odds and capture the presidency through creating a brand-new third party.

The presidential election unfolded in dramatic fashion in the Grand Rapids press and in conversations with neighbors and co-workers. The former president, formidable Republican Teddy Roosevelt, ran at the head of the Progressive "Bull Moose" party. Roosevelt grew up a child of wealthy New Yorkers but, like Roy, he courageously battled his own obstacles—being a sickly child who suffered from debilitating asthma. Roosevelt determined that the sickness could be overcome by a vigorous devotion to weightlifting and boxing. Having overcome his natural limitations, he determined to make something of himself. He entered politics and started climbing the ranks of the New York Assembly, but the tragic deaths of his mother and his wife on February 14, 1884, sent him reeling. He coped by leaving all that was familiar and living as a cowboy and cattle rancher for two years in the Dakota Territory. After mourning his wife and mother on the open ranges of the Dakotas and finding success capturing bandits in the west, he returned to New York. Unfulfilled by frontier exploits, he became police commissioner in New York City, and eventually US Navy Assistant Secretary under President William McKinley. When war broke out against Spain, he surrendered his post to organize a volunteer cavalry full of fellow enthusiasts aptly named "Rough Riders." This unorthodox band—a group of western cowboys, lawmen, and Ivy League associates— proved their metal in a bold charge up San Juan Hill in 1898, and catapulted their commander to fame and into the governor's mansion of New York the same year.

While the Republican Party leadership was pleased to have the governor's mansion, it was soon sorry for having to work with Roosevelt. The party leaders thought they could control him, but they couldn't have been more wrong. Roosevelt supported a tax on corporation franchises, he refused to serve big business interests, and he did not always serve party interests either. Roosevelt was charming and maddening, principled and opportunist, conservative and progressive.[5] Forced to regroup, the New York Republicans plotted to get rid of him by promotion and encouraged President McKinley to invite Roosevelt to join the ticket as candidate for vice president. McKinley warmed to the idea knowing that Roosevelt's charisma and standing in the West would be a huge asset to his campaign. While McKinley's advisors warned against Roosevelt, delegates at the 1899 Republican Convention, with the machinations of New York boss Thomas C. Platt, carried the day for Roosevelt.[6] Though Roosevelt understood that the position typically meant the end of a political career,[7] he

---

5. *Encyclopedia of American Biography*, eds. John A. Garraty and Jerome L. Sternstein (New York: Harper Collins, 1996), "Theodore Roosevelt."

6. Margaret Leech, *In the Days of McKinley* (New York: Harper and Brothers, 1959), 529–539.

7. One can usually prove this point by asking random observers who the VP was ten years ago. Wilson's Vice President Thomas Marshall's favorite quip was, "Once there were two brothers. One ran away to sea, the other was elected Vice-President, and neither of them was heard from again." Paul F. Boller Jr., *Presidential Campaigns* (New York: Oxford University Press, 1984), 199.

had a strong sense of duty to his country and enough hubris to believe he could use the position to his advantage. Tragedy struck soon after McKinley and Roosevelt won the 1900 Presidential elections, changing plans and destinies. A young Polish anarchist assassinated President McKinley and made Roosevelt president at the age of forty-two. There had never been a younger or more vigorous president. He pounded his fist on what he named the "bully" pulpit, he prosecuted monopolies, he constructed and sent a "Great White Fleet" around the world, and he negotiated the end of the Russo-Japanese War. After winning reelection in 1904, he declared that he would not run again. Eventually, circumstances and feelings made him reconsider midway through his handpicked successor's first term.

The current president in the election of 1912, Republican William Howard Taft, was born well, held an impeccable resume, and was destined to finish a distant third in this titanic struggle. Born in Cincinnati, Ohio, in 1857 to an influential Republican political family,[8] he spent his lifetime working through the family channels of law and political appointments. At Yale, his weight earned him the nickname "Big Lub," but he had the last laugh, winning the intramural heavyweight wrestling championship and graduating second in his class in 1878. He followed those triumphs with a Law degree in 1880, admission to the Ohio bar, and appointments to several posts including a judge of the Superior Court of Cincinnati in 1887. From the age of twenty-four to the last year of his life, he held one appointed public office after another. Only one office, the Presidency of the United States, did he gain by election, and even that election had more hallmarks of an appointment than

---

8. William's father Alfonso Taft served as Secretary of War and Attorney General under President Ulysses S. Grant.

something gained by vigorous effort. Taft simply got along well with other politicians, making him a capable administrator and problem solver. His competence, loyalty, and affability made him both a natural party man and logical appointee for higher and higher office. Following the brief Spanish-American War, President William McKinley needed someone to lead the commission to organize a civilian government in the newly acquired Philippines. Taft, well liked and respected in Republican circles, was a logical pick.[9] Taft explained to McKinley that he opposed the annexation of the islands, and he told the president that his real ambition was to serve on the Supreme Court. McKinley persisted, however, and Taft's acceptance of that role and his able administration made him popular with Americans and Filipinos alike. Taft continued to serve in the Philippines following McKinley's assassination and became an invaluable problem solver for McKinley's successor, Theodore Roosevelt. Taft's competent work in the Philippines, Cuba, Panama, Rome, and Japan earned him Roosevelt's gratitude and friendship, and Roosevelt offered Taft vacant positions on the Supreme Court when they came available. But Taft's sense of duty to unfinished work kept him from accepting. In 1907, Taft again indicated that he wanted to be Chief Justice of the Supreme Court, but there was no vacancy, and Roosevelt had grander plans for his loyal friend.

Taft didn't want the job (years later Taft wryly commented that he couldn't even remember being President of the United States). Regardless, Roosevelt, Taft's wife Helen, and his brother convinced

---

9. Taft recalled the conversation often as president. McKinley's final argument stated, "You don't want them any less than I do, but we have got them and in dealing with them I think I can trust the man who didn't want them better than I can the man who did." Margaret Leech, *In the Days of McKinley* (New York: Harper and Brothers, 1959), 484.

him it was his duty to accept the candidacy. Overshadowed from the beginning, Taft gave the impression that he was simply running to further implement Roosevelt's policies. Jokes circulated that T.A.F.T. meant "Take Advice from Theodore." Take advice he did, so that when Roosevelt told him to quit responding to Democratic nominee William Jennings Bryan and go on the attack, Taft complied. Roosevelt also advised him to continue talking about controlling big trusts and to stop playing elitist sports like golf and tennis when there were reporters around.[10] And Taft acquiesced.

While Roosevelt's direction and prestige ensured Taft's election in 1908, it could not save their friendship in the years that followed. Taft proved himself an able administrator as president, but he differed with Roosevelt over the proper use of executive power. After Taft fired an old friend of Roosevelt's, an influential senator wrote to Roosevelt complaining that Taft was undoing progressive gains, and Roosevelt took steps to reenter the political arena. By late 1911, the rift had widened further, and Roosevelt put himself forward as a candidate for the Republican nomination. An epic battle ensued between Roosevelt's charisma and Taft's political connections. The back-and-forth struggle culminated at the Republican convention. State conventions loyal to Taft ignored Roosevelt's primary wins and awarded the delegates to Taft. Roosevelt, recognizing that he could not win with the establishment making all the rules, decided to walk out, leading his followers out of the room singing "Onward Christian Soldiers." Roosevelt created his own party, the progressive Bull Moose Party, giving Republican

---

10. Paul F. Boller Jr., *Presidential Campaigns*, 188. Golf and tennis were considered elitist and didn't resonate with the common man. TR recommended horseback riding instead, but Taft's considerable weight was a problem.

voters two choices. While Taft and Roosevelt would reconcile before the latter's death, the two former and future friends pulled the Republican Party in two different directions which was nothing but good news for the serious, scholarly, well-spoken, Democratic nominee.

The future president in the election of 1912 was New Jersey Governor Woodrow Wilson. Wilson was born in the years immediately preceding the Civil War in Virginia, and raised by a thoughtful Presbyterian minister who cared greatly for the less fortunate. Like Roosevelt, he overcame serious disabilities. Where Roosevelt overcame physical obstacles, Wilson overcame mental ones: undiagnosed dyslexia prevented him from learning the alphabet until he was nine and from reading until he was eleven. Despite his slow start, Wilson caught up and surpassed his peers. He graduated from Princeton University, studied law at the University of Virginia, and finished his training in modern social sciences at Johns Hopkins. His doctoral dissertation, *Congressional Government*, explained the power of the congressional committees in the American system of government. His later book, *The State*, was the first textbook in comparative government and called for an activist government to address issues of the day. Wilson continued to write, and with the publication of *George Washington* in 1896 and his multi-volume *History of the United States*, Wilson became a popular author. Through this process, Wilson's ambition for a greater stage to apply what he had studied and taught for decades lingered. All he needed was a serious push.

In 1902, Wilson won the election to the presidency of Princeton and seized the opportunity to transform his quaint and venerable old school into a modern university. In education and politics, Wilson was both a practical, scientific reformer and a moral crusader. He wanted Princeton graduates to be skillful and righteous. He wanted to produce graduates who could understand and solve the general issues confronting the nation. To that end, Wilson threw himself into the task. He reorganized the curriculum, requiring students to major in a single subject and to follow an integrated course of study. His innovations replaced the chaos of the free-elective system which was then the norm of American higher education. In 1905, Wilson introduced the preceptorial system which effectively augmented lectures with systematic small-group discussions. This breakthrough was followed by an attempt to reconstruct Princeton into residential colleges. This was a bridge too far for the Dean of the Graduate school and many wealthy benefactors who preferred the current elitist social arrangements at the university. Wilson lost this fight but gained a reputation in New Jersey as one who fought for the common man against the power of privilege. Having run into a wall at Princeton, he began to seriously listen to those who had encouraged him to run for Governor of New Jersey.

Among those who wanted Wilson to run for governor were New Jersey Democratic bosses James Smith and George Harvey. Similar to the New York bosses who nominated Roosevelt, Smith and Harvey wanted to capitalize on reform sentiment without actually reforming. After sizing up Wilson, they believed they could control him. True, he told them in a meeting in New York, "If I were elected governor I should be very glad to consult with the leaders of the Democratic Organization. I should refuse to listen to no man, but I should be especially glad to hear and duly consider the suggestions of my party."[11] Still, they were used to winks, nods,

---

11. Quoted in William Bayard Hale, *Woodrow Wilson: The Story of His Life* (Garden City, N.Y.: Doubleday, 1912), 168–169.

fine-sounding words, and no real action. Wilson was speaking very precisely though—he would consider their suggestions, but he would not obey their dictates. He was a Princeton man after all, and like the hundreds he had trained, he would be a skillful, righteous servant of the people. After being elected governor, he enacted a variety of progressive reforms including workmen's compensation, direct primaries, school reforms, and the regulation of public utilities. This thoroughly frustrated the machine, but he was a popular governor, and they hoped they could wait him out. After all, he had greater ambitions than being Governor of New Jersey. When the Democrats looked for a reform candidate for the 1912 election, Wilson was a natural choice. With the help of thrice-defeated William Jennings Bryan, Wilson's backers at the Democratic Convention outlasted the backers of conservative Alton B. Parker and party regular and Speaker of the House, Champ Clark. The Democrats had nominated a progressive, a man who embodied the spirit of the age. Reading the signs of the times and the divided nature of their opponents, they rightly believed the election was theirs to lose.

Like most elections in US history, the participants described it as historic and pivotal. Roy certainly had never seen anything like it. Roosevelt declared weeks after he left the Republican Party,

To you men and women who have come here to this great city of this great State formally to launch a new party, a party of the people of the whole Union, the National Progressive party, I extend my hearty greeting. You are taking a bold and a greatly needed step for the service of our beloved country. The old parties are husks, with no real soul within either, divided on artificial lines, boss-ridden and privilege-controlled, each a jumble of incongruous elements, and neither daring to speak out wisely and fearlessly what should be said on the vital issues of the day.[12]

"Boss-ridden and privilege-controlled" meant that the people could not rule themselves in the current system. Roosevelt called for presidential primaries and the direct election of US Senators. He called for the exposure of corrupt practices and transparency in campaign contributions. He called for honest judges and humane working conditions, including a work week that included one day of rest out of seven and shifts that were no longer than twelve hours a day. Most of all, he claimed to be the true progressive in the race and finished the speech with a call to sacrifice and determination, concluding with, "We stand at Armageddon, and we battle for the Lord."[13]

Wilson and Taft did not talk of Armageddon. While Wilson referred to Roosevelt as "a very, very erratic comet now sweeping across our horizon,"[14] He primarily talked about his program of progressive reform labeled the "New Freedom." Events tended to overshadow words, however. On October 14, a fanatic named John Shrank stepped up, shouted something about a third term, and shot Roosevelt in the breast. Roosevelt, stumbling, cried out to the crowd who was pummeling the assassin, "Stand back. Don't hurt the man!"[15] Having saved the assassin's life, he then paid no

---

12. Theodore Roosevelt, "A Confession of Faith: We Stand at Armageddon, and We Battle for the Lord." Progressive Party Convention—Chicago, Illinois, August 6, 1912. http://www.theodore-roosevelt.com/images/research/speeches/trarmageddon.pdf, accessed July 7, 2013.

13. Roosevelt, "A Confession of Faith."

14. John Milton Cooper Jr., *The Warrior and the Priest*, (Cambridge: Belknap, 1983), 139. Roosevelt's return had coincided with Halley's comet in 1910.

15. J.C. Furnas, *The Americans: A Social History of the United States 1587-1914* (New York: G.P. Putnam's Sons, 1969), 864.

attention to his own. Brushing aside his worried physicians, he rode to the auditorium and insisted on giving his planned speech. When he reached the hall, someone announced that he had been shot. Roosevelt quieted the standing, anxious crowd with a wave and managed out a harsh whisper that it was true, he had been shot, but he would continue. He took out his manuscript from his pocket, red and soaked with blood. The crowd gasped, but he reassured them he was not hurt badly and had something to say. "I have had an A-1 time in life and I am having it now." He blamed the critics for stirring up fanatics,[16] and delivered his hour-and-a-half speech.

The doctors later marveled that he survived, crediting his powerful muscles that prevented the bullet from piercing his lung. Still, he had a fractured rib and a bullet embedded near his lung. In sympathy, Wilson and Taft suspended their campaigns until Roosevelt could continue. Their act was more than a noble gesture, though. Wilson was exhausted from all the campaigning and believed he had a comfortable lead. Taft believed he had no chance of victory; he told a friend in July 1912, "I think I might as well give up so far as being a candidate is concerned. There are so many in the country who don't like me."[17] Weeks later, Taft's fears and Roosevelt's concerns came to pass. Wilson won on November 5th in a landslide victory, carrying forty of the forty-eight states. Wilson only won 41.9 percent of the popular vote, but in a three

---

16. Furnas, *The Americans*, 864. Roosevelt had seen this before. Hearst had so hated McKinnley he allowed writers in his papers to call for violence against the president. A staff editorial read six months before McKinley's assassination, "If bad institutions and bad men can be got rid of only by killing them, then the killing must be done."

17. Henry F. Pringle, *The Life and Times of William Howard Taft, 2 vols* (New York: Farrar and Rinehart, 1939), II, 809.

way battle he triumphed. The Democrats captured both houses of Congress and twenty-one governorships. Wilson, the president who would send Roy off to France, had been elected. Certainly, no one expected Wilson to have to concentrate much on foreign policy, let alone lead the US into a World War.

Curiously missing in all the eloquent speeches and carefully outlined positions of the campaign of 1912 was any serious talk of foreign policy or the approaching possibilities of war. Roosevelt had warned of an upcoming battle and had been half right. He had imagined a domestic struggle between privilege and the people. The real Armageddon was coming to the battlefields in Europe. Few could perceive that, however. Only little and unimportant Serbia warranted mention as a hot spot in the news.[18] The Americans historically could ignore European struggles for power and dominance. After all, the Atlantic Ocean had long protected the US from involvement in the wars of Europe. Neither the common man like Roy, nor the educated elite like Roosevelt or Wilson could foresee that the vast blue moat could not keep the US in isolation this time.

---

18. Newspapers made predictions for the coming year each December. Even as late as December 1913, newspaper opinion writers happily declared the world was peaceful except a simmering conflict in the Balkans.

★ ★ ★ ★ ★

Approaching the Unthinkable

*It would be an irony of fate if my administration
had to deal with foreign problems, for all my preparation
has been in domestic matters.*
—Woodrow Wilson, 1912

★ ★ ★ ★ ★

ORLD WAR WAS as far from President Wilson's mind as it was from Roy's in March, 1913. While Roy supported his family with long hours as an unskilled farmhand, Wilson was forging his first year as president. He had only mentioned foreign affairs in passing during his campaign. How could he possibly be conscious of the complex forces propelling the world toward war? Yet, he was one of those forces, although not at first. The new president started out determined not to call young men like Roy to end a destructive European war, but rather to call Congress to resolve the problems created by powerful private businesses and inept government.

Wilson's groundbreaking election forced change. He became the first Democrat to occupy the White House since Roy's birth and the first elected president of Southern origin since before the Civil War. He was of a different political persuasion than most of Roy's Republican neighbors, but strove to persuade them to join him anyway.[1] The United States was his battleground. In his short inaugural address, Wilson proposed that the United States had been given a new start, championing a system of government that gave citizens a new freedom, and he framed the battle as a fight between good and evil. According to Wilson, the rich and the powerful had taken advantage of the poor and powerless, and the government had callously ignored the desperate problems of

---

1. "Republican Control of Legislature is Assured but Margin is Narrow," *Detroit Free Press*, 7 November 1912.

ordinary citizens.[2] Wilson proposed that the time had come for the federal government to right the wrongs.

Wilson approached these daunting domestic issues as a progressive. Progressives believed that humans could conquer disease, poverty, and other persistent troubles that plagued the human race since the beginning of recorded time. Their faith in the power of empirical science, a liberal arts education, and the essential goodness of mankind knew almost no limit.[3] With confidence, Wilson began checking off, one by one, the long list of domestic issues demanding his attention. Breaking precedent with every president since Jefferson, he addressed Congress in person and performed his duties more in line with a leader in Great Britain's parliament than a US President. The results were spectacular. The Underwood Tariff (1913) reduced duties and provided for a graduated income tax on personal incomes. The Federal Reserve Act (1913) created an elastic currency and divided the nation into twelve banking districts. In 1914, he convinced Congress to pass the Clayton Act and establish the Federal Trade Commission, both of which investigated and regulated corporations.[4] This success in progressive legislation within his first eighteen months achieved what other progressive leaders like Grover Cleveland, Roosevelt, and Taft could not. Wilson believed that these broad legislative initiatives would be significant steps toward reducing inequality and providing more opportunities and protections for citizens like

2. Ray Stannard Baker, *Woodrow Wilson: Life and Letters,* Potomac ed. vol. 3 (New York: Charles Scribner's Sons, 1946), 10.

3. Arthur Link, *Woodrow Wilson and the Progressive Era: 1910-1917* (New York: Harper and Brothers, 1954), 2.

4. Kendrick A. Clements, *Woodrow Wilson: World Statesman* (Boston: Twayne, 1987), 233.

Roy at the bottom rung in society. Of course, these changes were structural and, even if successful, would take time to trickle down to the average worker.

Meanwhile, miles outside Grand Rapids, Roy worked long hours for minimal wages. In vain, he looked for work that would pay enough to support himself and be a significant source of help to his family, but he simply didn't have the skills or connections to advance. He asked his friends for leads, asked Pearl to inquire about openings around town, and even tried boxing. On the surface, he kept it light with jokes and positivity, but deep down, he was deeply dissatisfied. Roy missed his family on those long days working the farm and other jobs. Sometimes, he imagined himself finally trudging the rutted road home only to find the house empty and his family gone, like his father, never to be seen again.[5] "Please tell me if the family relocates," he begged Pearl.

While Roy tried unsuccessfully to figure out what work he would do in the coming years, newspaper writers attempted to analyze the present and predict the future. The *New York Times* article "Noteworthy Events in the World's Progress in 1913" chronicled both the ongoing conflict in the Balkans and the steep increase in military budgets for Germany and France. Despite those signs of tension, the Times believed disagreements between great powers were small and getting better. Even the Russians seemed to have remarkable stability. On the eve of the end of all that was familiar, they happily celebrated the three-hundredth anniversary of the Romanoff dynasty throughout their vast country. Europe was at peace, and was likely to be at peace in the coming year, or so it seemed at the end of 1913.

---

5. Clark Blanchard, interview by the author, August 4, 2000.

As Europe wandered closer and closer to the cliff, Americans busied themselves with getting on and getting ahead. Signs of progress were everywhere. If you lived in Tampa Bay or St. Petersburg, Florida, you could now fly across the bay for five dollars. Henry Ford had recently stabilized his assembly line turnover by doubling employees' wages and shortening their work day by an hour. Now, Ford assembly-line workers made five dollars per eight-hour day, worked five days a week, and could afford the cars they produced. The casual observer of the assembly line saw a moving monstrosity of chains and links and parts that moved through the room in a series of eighty-four steps. The mass-produced, interchangeable parts enabled assembly in a speedy and organized fashion. The chassis of the car was pulled down the 150 foot line by a chain conveyor, and the 140 workers all did their jobs on the line, supplied by additional workers who brought the parts to them so they could stay focused and on the line. What had taken twelve hours the year before now took ninety-three minutes. The only color that could dry in that short time was black, but the lack of color options didn't slow sales. Ford sold 248,000 cars in 1914.

One place worth driving to in 1914 was the movie theater. Film critics in the important trade magazine, *The Moving Picture World*, reviewed one film with a "clever player who takes the role of the nervy and very nifty sharper in this picture is a comedian of the first water who acts like one of Nature's own naturals . . . . People out for an evening's good time will howl."[6] The film was titled *Making a Living*, and the impoverished gentleman dressed in a top hat, frock coat, and monocle, sporting a drooping mustache,

---

6. Moving Picture World, Jan-Mar 1914, 678, http://lantern.mediahist.org/catalog/movingpicturewor19newy_0704, accessed July 1, 2016.

was twenty-four-year-old, England-born actor Charlie Chaplin performing in his first film.

Amid the material progress for those who could afford plane rides, automobiles, and movies, President Wilson wrapped up his legislative triumphs for those who could not. As he and the progressives celebrated their historic achievements, tragedy struck. It didn't seem serious at first. On a cold March day, President Wilson's wife, Ellen, slipped and fell on the polished floor of her White House bedroom. Weeks later, she was still confined to her bed. Whether it was the result of her fall or of the strain of being first lady, neither Ellen nor the president knew. They later learned that the fall had coincided with a more serious ailment. Ellen suffered from Bright's disease, a serious kidney ailment from which she would not recover. As spring and summer passed, Wilson stayed attentive to his wife, while his worries for her and the rest of the world increased exponentially.

Like Ellen, the world was much less healthy than it had appeared. While some popular writers, thinkers, and politicians had become convinced that progress and education had shown the Western world the folly of war, others were not so sure. The competition, intense rivalry, and fear of an ascendant Germany following the Franco-Prussian War placed the major powers in precarious positions.

In 1870, decades before Roy was born and Wilson took office, France was still considered the dominant military power in Europe. In fact, the Napoleonic wars had taught Europe that only when they gathered as a whole could they defeat France. So, when German Statesman Otto Von Bismarck provoked a fight with mighty France, everyone rightly expected a quick conflict. They assumed wrongly, however, that mighty France would make rapid work of disorganized Germany.

Germany in 1870 was no longer disorganized,[7] and the French should have recognized the signs. Instead of clear sight, they had supreme confidence in the descendants of those who had brought Europe to its knees during the Napoleonic wars. The French had courage, training, and a grand tradition. Their uniforms were the most magnificent in Europe, their rifles and pre-machine guns were superior to the German's, and their emperor had published two treatises on artillery. Moreover, the French didn't have the deciding military advantage that belonged to the Germans with their superior cannons made from the innovative steelworks of Krupp.

Made of bronze, the French cannons loaded slowly. Though accurate, they didn't have half the range of German cannons, which were fashioned with the finest steel. Germany also had extensive railroads, designed with artillery and troop mobilization in mind.

Aware of French strengths, the Germans took out the French machine guns in the first salvo, staying safely out of range and shelling the French until they broke and ran. The French retreated to their ancient fortresses and set their cannons at the walls, but could not withstand the German shells.

German troops then surrounded Paris. Paris responded by voting in a new government, which sent out instructions to the troops by balloon. French troops sent back panicked responses by carrier pigeons, and the Germans countered by releasing hawks. The leader of the French Republic, also feeling pursued, slipped out of Paris in

---

7. Their victory against the Austrians in 1866 hinted at this fact. Looking back at German military strikes in 1870, 1914, and 1939, it seems that the nations of Europe should have foreseen the ferocity of German aggression in each instance.

a hot air balloon. Like a series of dominos, France fell. On October 27, French Marshal Bazaine surrendered at Metz with 173,000 men. Paris, under siege and eating a diet of cats, dogs, and rats, gave in on January 19, 1871. The Treaty of Frankfurt, signed on May 10, 1871, ceded territory to Germany and agreed to pay a heavy indemnity to the victors.

The German victory shocked the French and distressed the watching English and Russians. All three major powers decided that their future security depended on forging a new alliance to contain Germany and its ally Austria-Hungary. This alliance, known as the Triple Entente,[8] intended to safeguard all three powers against German aggression. In reality, it gave all a false sense of security and ensured that any small conflict on the European continent would quickly escalate into a World War. The Germans, led by an authoritarian and militaristic Kaiser Wilhelm, took pride in their growing power and prestige following the Franco-Prussian War. The Germans were also keenly aware that the French, British, and Russians would work side by side to keep them contained.

Further stoking the conflict was the popular idea of Social Darwinism. Inspired by Charles Darwin's theory of evolution, scientists fitted evidence to a general theory of eugenics in an attempt to identify which races were the most fit. This pseudo-science led to genetic screening, birth control, marriage restrictions, segregation, compulsory sterilization, forced abortions, and, in the worst cases, attempted genocide in order to get rid of what they believed to be undesirable races. The question of who was superior among the European powers, however, went beyond eugenics. Leaders in Britain, France, Germany, and, in some cases,

---

8. French for "friendship."

America believed gaining colonies and territory was not only a way to gain natural resources and trading partners, but also a way to prove they were the most fit. Survival of the fittest makes for dangerous foreign policy and, when combined with national pride, it resulted in a mad dash for colonies from 1880 until 1914. The great powers of Europe embarked on a global competition to prove their supremacy. In the last quarter of the 19th century, Africa was almost completely divided into European dependencies. Colonial powers divided China like a giant melon, and Southeast Asia was largely colonized by the Dutch, French, and British. The world, aside from Japan and the Americas, appeared to be firmly in the grip of European powers. Fear of Germany, competition between nations, and a massive buildup of armaments set the stage. The world waited like a powder keg.

In June of 1914, Serbian nationalists lit the match. Five young Serbs and a Bosnian Muslim, all part of the clandestine organization known as the Black Hand, waited for a Habsburg Prince, hoping to spark a Serbian revolution to overthrow the hated Austrians. They knew he was coming to Sarajevo to watch military maneuvers.

Archduke Franz Ferdinand, nephew to the Emperor, was traveling to the residence of the providential governor with his wife in the car when he was spotted by a member of the Black Hand. The assassin threw a bomb at the car, but it bounced off. Forty-five minutes later, the Archduke was en route to visit an officer injured in the failed bombing attempt when his chauffer took a wrong turn, stopped, and turned the car around. While the car was at a momentary halt, Gavrilo Princip, a small nineteen-year-old Yugoslav nationalist, stepped forward, took aim, and shot twice, hitting first the Archduke in the neck and then his wife Sophie when she bravely tried to shield her husband from the assassin. Princip then swallowed what he believed was a fatal dose of cyanide. The pill, however, only made him sick; he survived the day, eventually stood trial, and lived long enough to see the world descend into total war. The Archduke and his wife only lived a few more hours.

The anger and tension spread faster than anyone could anticipate. In a matter of days, the investigation into the assassination determined that the conspirators were supported and equipped by the Serbian military. Unfortunately for peace and progress, the Serbians also were strongly supported by the Russians who shared their Orthodox faith. These two facts made military action against Serbia complicated. Therefore, Austria sought their ally Germany's advice and partnership in the matter.

Once Austria consulted Germany, the situation became a global issue.[9] France, Russia, and Britain had signed treaties to contain Germany. Germany had signed treaties to keep themselves from being contained. The Austrians, allied with the Germans, were anxious to keep the various peoples in their empire from gaining independence. The Russians, allied with the French and the British, were eager to show the world that they would not let their Slavic brethren in Serbia be bullied. Each major power was determined

---

9. Keegan, 52. France agreed to go to war on Russia's side and vice versa if either were attacked by Germany, Britain to lend assistance to France if the vital interests of both were judged threatened. Germany, Austria-Hungary and Italy (The Triple Alliance) to go to war together if anyone were attacked by two other states . . . At their worst, those consequences would bring Russia to threaten Austria on their common border as a warning to desist from action against Serbia; Austria would then look to Germany for support; that support, if given, risked drawing France into the crisis as a counterweight against Germany's pressure on Russia. The combination of Russia would supply the circumstances to activate the Triple alliance (with or without Italy); the ingredients of a general European war would then be in place.

to prove its Darwinian fitness, certain of its cultural and military supremacy, and confident in the well-planned alliances.

The Serbians, not fully understanding the precarious world situation, were tired of foreign rule and sought advice from the British, Russian, and French ministers on whether or not to give in to Austria's demands. A last minute note from Russia strengthened their resolve. The Serbians attached conditions to six of Austria's demands and rejected outright the demand that Austrian officials be allowed to take part in the investigation of the assassinations on Serbian territory. The Austrian diplomatic legation received the note and left Belgrade immediately. In the confusion, distraction, and incomplete understanding that followed, no successful attempt to arrange a great-power conference materialized.

The chaos led to reckless decisions. Austria declared war on Serbia on July 28, 1914, hoping to knock them out of the war quickly and swing the bulk of their limited forces around to the inevitable Russian advance. Russia responded by ordering a general mobilization on July 29. Troops were mustered, young men said goodbye to their families, and trains began to move toward enemy borders. In the midst of the mobilization, cousins Tsar Nicholas II of Russia and Kaiser Wilhelm II sent telegrams back and forth, but could not stop the militarists who were frightened of losing any advantage through delay.

President Wilson received reports daily and offered to mediate, but was ignored by the European powers. On August 1, Germany ordered general mobilization. France's military leaders sent the Minister of War a note that pointed out the reason for the hurry. France's military experts calculated that, with every twenty-four hours of delay, they would lose fifteen to twenty-five kilometers of territory. Since the Germans were sending soldiers and equipment to the front by train, France had no time to lose and put its own mobilization in motion. Frantically, cousins Nicholas and Wilhelm conferred via telegram, begging each other not to violate each other's territory. Britain dithered on the sidelines, refusing to give clarifying answers to either France or Germany. Acting on a decades-old war plan, Germany delivered an ultimatum to Belgium on August 2, demanding the use of its territory in operations against France. The next day, Germany began operations against Belgium and declared war on France, claiming that French aircraft had violated its territory. Britain, who had an ancient treaty with Belgium guaranteeing its neutrality, stopped dithering and formally joined France and Russia with a declaration of war against Germany at midnight August 5. World War I had begun.

Ironically, in the madness of treaties and mobilization timetables, the war passed by Serbia in 1914. The Serbs, the originators of the conflict, were strategically irrelevant and would not see war for fourteen months.

Helpless to stop the events in Europe, Wilson could do little but write letters to foreign powers while he sat anxiously by Ellen's side. He could not help his wife either. As the nations of the world stumbled toward total war, Ellen passed away. The president went days without sleep and wept uncontrollably at her burial in Rome, Georgia.

Physically removed and emotionally drained, Wilson declared that the US stood neutral and apart from the conflict. Like most Americans, Wilson believed that with the Atlantic Ocean between the US and Europe, America could resist getting pulled into the deadly conflict.[10] The other uncomfortable reality was that even if Wilson had wanted to pick a side to aid in World War I, the US military was wholly unprepared.

---

10. Link, *Woodrow Wilson and the Progressive Era*, 267–282.

The signs of unpreparedness had long been there for anyone to notice. The Spanish-American War of 1898, while ultimately successful, convinced experts that the military could not defeat a first-rate power.[11] This truth spurred leaders like Theodore Roosevelt to call for preparedness, and representatives in Congress to move forward with plans for modernization and expansion of the military. The World War only strengthened their resolve and increased their urgency. Proponents of this idea of preparedness argued that, not only would an improved military protect US interests abroad, it could provide jobs to the young men like Roy in the US.

Joblessness had reached alarming rates in the US and had attracted enough attention that a National Conference on Unemployment met earlier in the year before the crisis in Europe materialized. Delegates from twenty-five states and fifty-nine cities came to the conference and discussed current issues as well as the chronic problem of joblessness that they believed inherent in an industrial society.[12] The downturn that had begun in 1913 hit major industries in the Midwest particularly hard. Later, unions in Roy's part of the country reported heavy unemployment, merely one symptom of the worst depression since the 1890s.[13]

What was bad for industrial workers was even worse for sixteen year-old Roy Blanchard, who worked long hours and sometimes tried to hold down two jobs at once.[14] He had little time for leisure,

---

11. John J. Pershing, *My Experiences in the World War* (New York: Frederick A. Stokes, 1931), 6–14.

12. Edward Robb Ellis, *Echoes of Distant Thunder: Life in the United States, 1914-1918* (New York: Kodansha, 1996), 54.

13. John M. Cooper, *Pivotal Decades* (New York: W.W. Norton, 1990), 211.

14. Roy Blanchard, Letter to Pearl Blanchard, 21 July 1915, Roy Blanchard papers, Grand Rapids, MI.

managing to earn just enough money to keep body and soul together. Farming wasn't the answer, and his desperation drove Roy to look elsewhere.[15]

He found his answer in February, 1916, when a friend mentioned the National Guard. The Guard paid better than the odd jobs he'd been getting and promised relief from tedious farm work. Hoping he'd worked his last day on a farm, he signed the appropriate line and made his oath.

The military that Roy joined did not yet inspire widespread confidence. Educators lamented that the problem with military instruction was that it led either to nowhere or to trouble. Other branches of instruction led men to useful professions, but military training had no social value or any other redeeming feature.[16] Chief of Staff Hugh L. Scott acknowledged this negative image and worked to promote the positive aspects of service—namely, that the stabilizing effect of military discipline and intensive training would form character and provide a foundation for the enlistees' life's work. Facing the challenges inherent in military life would give young men sincere patriotism: a sense of duty and responsibility that would benefit the nation as a whole. For leaders like Douglas MacArthur, this high mission justified even occasionally rough and severe treatment. Judges, believing that this process worked well, sometimes even released men without punishment if they would enter the Army.[17]

If the country felt general contempt for the regular army in 1915,

---

15. Ibid., 28 July 1915.

16. Penn Borden, *Civilian Indoctrination of the Military: World War I and Future Implications for the Military-Industrial Complex* (New York: Greenwood, 1989), 2.

17. Ibid., 2–4.

the army felt even more animosity for the National Guard. Although it was considered a reserve force, most officers in the regular army considered the National Guard as practically worthless.

People in the Midwest didn't think much of soldiers, and they thought even less of war in general. In Roy's time, Michigan was firmly anti-interventionist. The newspapers mentioned the European conflict every day, but the very makeup of the Midwest prevented significant support for US involvement on either side. In 1903, sixty percent of male voters in the state of Michigan were either immigrants or the sons of immigrants. Having left a troubled and contentious Europe behind, they believed wars were the result of imperialism and power politics, and they wanted no part of either. They also had no desire to see the United States fight their old country or, worse, to face relatives on the battlefield if they were drafted. The following quote summarizes the feelings of the Midwest farmer:

> We will—every man of us—fight in a minute if the country is invaded, but we won't go a step farther. We'd keep every American off belligerent ships. We'd keep every American out of Mexico. We'd let the Japs take the Philippines and be damned, if they wanted 'em. We'd defend our homes, but when any American goes where he has no right to go, if he gets into trouble, it's his own fault. The honor of the country doesn't get outside our boundaries that we can see.[18]

Ignoring the Army's disdain and the isolationist sentiment, Roy left his farm tools at home and signed up with the National Guard. His recruiter promised job training, athletics, dances, and target

---

18. *Literary Digest,* February 12, 1916. Quoted in Billington, "The Origins of Middle Western Isolationism," 55.

practice—there was little threat of battle. Roy was joining the *Michigan* National Guard, after all, and certainly no one believed Canada would invade. The idea of having to defend the US borders against foreign invaders seemed ludicrous.

But the world had gone mad, and not just in Europe. In Mexico, a bandit named Pancho Villa was preparing a raid across the border into Texas, hoping against all odds to unite Mexico by attacking the United States. Roy didn't know it at the time, but, when he volunteered for the National Guard, he was signing up to strap on a side arm and guard the US-Mexican border.

CHAPTER 3

★ ★ ★ ★ ★

SECURING
THE BORDER

*LUSITANIA SUNK BY A SUBMARINE, PROBABLY 1,260
DEAD; TWICE TORPEDOED OFF IRISH COAST; SINKS
IN 15 MINUTES; CAPT. TURNER SAVED, FROHMAN
AND VANDERBILT MISSING; WASHINGTON
BELIEVES THAT A GRAVE CRISIS IS AT HAND.*
—New York Times, May 8, 1915

*At two o clock I heard a rustle in the bushes and halted
something. "It" didn't halt so up went the gat[1] and
it swore a red blaze.*
—Roy Blanchard to Pearl Blanchard, 2 September
1916, Fort Hancock, Texas-Mexico Border

---

1. This was a slang name for a soldier's revolver.

★ ★ ★ ★ ★

While Roy was busy securing work, President Wilson worked to keep the US out of the war. Since the troubled days of the prelude to World War in July and August of 1914, Wilson had both offered himself as a mediator and taken concrete steps to keep the United States out of the war. Neither assignment turned out to be easy. Wilson's offers to mediate went unanswered and the US was too connected with Europe socially and economically to keep totally out of the conflict. The most difficult issue to navigate was the blockade.

Britain believed blockading Germany was a legitimate military strategy. Certainly, the Americans understood: the North had successfully blockaded the South in the American Civil War. Britain's Navy was sizable and in firm control of the seas. If they suspected that an American vessel carried contraband to the Central Powers, the British Navy intercepted the vessel, took it to the nearest port and investigated the cargo. While Americans expressed irritation at the inconvenience, no one lost their lives. Germany, however, had a much smaller Navy and could not follow the accepted rules of search and seizure of a neutral vessel. The only way it could keep supplies from getting to Britain was by sinking the ship via U-boat with a surprise torpedo. The U-boats were essentially submersible ships with limited mobility while submerged. Even while surfaced, they could not keep pace with either commercial or military vessels on the high seas. They could, nevertheless, take down any ship with a single torpedo, and proved that repeatedly throughout the war. In 1914, three Allied and neutral ships were sunk. This increased to 396 in 1915. No one was safe. Cargo ships, Red Cross vessels, even clearly marked relief ships for Belgium sank straight to the bottom.

Countermeasures against submarines were only partially successful. Armed merchant vessels showed Germans they couldn't afford to surface and let the crews disembark. The hydrophone attempted to listen for subs, but it had limited effect. The 1916 British development of the depth charge, an industrial drum filled with explosives and fitted with a pressure sensitive fuse, had some success but could not provide consistent protection. Laughing at the countermeasures, the Germans sank 964 ships in 1916. The best strategy that the Allied and neutral countries came up with to avoid being sunk was to go full speed, plotting an unpredictable zigzag course.

From the beginning of the war, influential politicians in Germany warned against the danger of enraging neutrals like the US through unrestricted submarine warfare. Militarists countered that sinking ships full of supplies intended for their enemies made it worth the risk. In January of 1915, a German submarine destroyed the *William P. Frye* that was transporting wheat from Seattle to England; March of the same year they torpedoed the *Falaba,* taking one American life. On May 1, a German U-boat torpedoed the American tanker *Gulflight.* The pressure on President Wilson as he tried to navigate peace without giving away the United States' freedom of the seas was enormous. He confessed, "I go to bed completely exhausted."[2] Ultimately, nothing would try German's insecurity or drain Wilson's stamina like the *Lusitania* tragedy on May 7, 1915. Roy read about the tragedy in the papers, but thousands experienced it firsthand.

On the morning of Friday May 7, 1915, the *Lusitania* broke

2. A. Scott Berg, *Wilson* (New York: G.P. Putnam's Sons, 2013), 354–355.

through the fog into the sunshine drenched North Atlantic. Captain William Thomas Turner, commodore of the Cunard fleet, knew that the German government had declared the seas around the British Iles to be a war zone. He knew he was carrying nearly 2,000 souls, but he also knew that he was carrying, among other things, a shipment of bullets, three-inch shells, and fuses. He believed that his top possible speed of twenty-one knots made the 1907 record-setter nearly invulnerable to the much slower German U-boats who had been sighted in the area. Nonetheless, in order to be responsible, he had fitted the ship for emergencies, including doubling the watch, closing the watertight doors, swinging out the lifeboats, and blacking out the ship. He was not, however, zigzagging the ship.

Captain Turner focused on the sub-threat alone. Since the *Lusitania* had broken through the fog, he increased the ship's speed to eighteen knots. At 11:55, he received a message from the British Admiralty: "SUBMARINE ACTIVE IN SOUTHERN PART OF IRISH CHANNEL, LAST HEARD OF TWENTY MILES SOUTH OF CONINGBEG LIGHT VESSEL." At 12:10 he abruptly altered the ship's course twenty degrees to port. The turn was sudden enough to jar many passengers off balance.

German U-boat Captain Lieutenant Walther Schwieger patrolled the west and south coasts of Ireland. In the last two days, he had sunk three merchant vessels. Throughout his career, he would sink forty-nine targets, making him the sixth most successful U-boat Captain in the war. He only had three torpedoes left, though, and he had orders to save two for the dangerous trip home.

At 12:40, Captain Turner received another message from the Admiralty. This one warned of a submarine five miles south of Cape Clear, proceeding west. Turner wrongly believed the *Lusitania* was now in the clear.

The passengers were tense, commoner and aristocrat alike. Dr. C.E. Foss walked on the port side of "A" deck, looking at the Irish coast in the distance. He joined a small group of passengers who talked singularly about the coast and the threat of attack by U-boats, which had incidentally been a constant source of conversation since they had left New York. They had all seen or heard of the threats that the German government had posted in American newspapers, warning passengers that they entered a war zone at their own risk. Suddenly, Dr. Foss saw a submarine rise to the surface about a mile away and steam parallel with the ship. He figured the *Lusitania* must have been going slower than top speed since the submarine kept pace for around five minutes. Asking the other passengers to keep an eye on the threat, he grabbed his glasses from the smoking room. Confirming his fears, he handed his glasses to a nearby sailor. Moments later the submarine dived below the surface. The *Lusitania* then swerved, giving Dr. Foss the impression the captain had also seen the submarine. The spooked passengers went to the giant two-decked saloon and tried to calm their nerves over lunch.[3]

The bridge had not seen the submarine. The swerve was the *Lusitania* reverting to South 87 East. Captain Turner gave instructions for a four-point bearing and left the bridge and headed to the chartroom in order to plot a course through the channel into Queenstown harbor.

Schwieger had spotted the large ship twenty minutes previously. Astounded by his luck, he submerged the U-20 and plotted an intercept course. The pilot took careful notes as he examined the ship through the periscope—four funnels, a huge ship upwards of 20,000 tons, making twenty-two knots (twenty-five mph)—

---

3. "Survivor Here Saw Trap for Lusitania," *New York Times,* May 25, 1915.

it had to be either the *Lusitania* or the *Mauretania*. The U-20 prepared for action, and at a range of 650 yards, fired off a G6 torpedo from a forward tube. The torpedo cleared the tube and streaked toward the *Lusitania* at over forty-two mph at the depth of nine feet.

Captain Turner returned to the bridge. From the crow's nest came the warning, "Torpedo coming on the starboard side!" Almost immediately the *Lusitania* shuddered and the bridge heard a sound like a giant heavy door being slammed shut. Virtually instantaneously, a second, much larger explosion rocked the ship—a tall column of water and debris shot skyward. Fearing the worst, Turner immediately sent an SOS and turned the *Lusitania* toward the coast of Ireland, hoping that he could beach the vessel; but the ship was already listing. The engines simply drove more water into the hull.

The passengers were momentarily stunned into shock. Most of them had only minutes more to live. Dr. Foss looked from side to side, his heart sinking with the ship as he felt the gradual list to starboard. Recovering from the initial shock, he ran up the companionway to the deck from the dining saloon. He saw some of the crew taking lifebelts from boxes lashed to the deck and fitting them on themselves. Passengers everywhere were looking frantically for lifebelts. Dr. Foss headed down to his cabin where he had left his lifebelt, but the list of the boat was now too severe. Six minutes after the explosion, the bow of the boat was already under water. He wasn't going to make it to his cabin, and most of the lifeboats were not going to be successfully launched.

The damage caused by one torpedo also shocked the German submarine captain. He noted the "unusually heavy detonation," and a second explosion due to unknown causes. He then brought the periscope down and directed the U-20 back to sea.[4]

Dr. Foss frantically searched for a lifebelt as the 787-foot ship fell apart. One of the huge funnels fell down onto the deck with a terrific crash. Avoiding the debris and weaving through the chaos, he managed to get one of the lifebelts from a box on deck. Getting on a lifeboat proved immoral—the boats in the vicinity would not even have enough space for the women and children. His fate decided, he jumped over the starboard side aft into the water. Hitting the water feet first, he found himself immediately in further peril. Immediately after he jumped, a five-ton lifeboat had fallen off the listing deck and came over the side straight at him. The boat landed feet from him and immediately capsized. The five men in the foundering boat pitched out. One couldn't swim fast enough to avoid the pull of the starboard wing propeller. Dr. Foss managed to get him clear of the propeller with a rope, but his legs were nearly severed and he bled out quickly.[5]

Not all the men fled the doomed ship. In the nursery, Alfred Vanderbilt—one of the world's richest men—and playwright Carl Frohman tied life jackets to wicker "Moses baskets" holding infants in an attempt to save them from going down with the ship. The baskets gave the infants only a few last moments. The rising water carried them off the boat, but none got clear of the turbulence and

4. http://en.wikipedia.org/wiki/Walther_Schwieger, accessed Feb 15, 2014. He would arrive in Germany to a hero's welcome. He would spend the next two years sinking enemy vessels. His next command would be over U88, which wreaked havoc for thirteen months before striking a British mine north of Terchelling. His body remains entombed with the rest of his crew in U-88.

5. "Survivor Here Saw Trap for Lusitania," *New York Times*, May 25, 1915, http://militaryhistory.about.com/od/worldwar1/p/lusitania.htm, accessed Feb 15, 2014.

were dragged down with the *Lusitania*. Vanderbilt and Frohman were never seen again.[6] Captain Turner stayed at his post until the end, eventually being swept overboard with the bridge crew as the *Lusitania* plunged beneath the waves, her propellers straight up in the air and churning wildly, sinking quickly from view a mere eighteen minutes after being struck by the single torpedo. As the ship vanished, the water was dotted with the bodies of the dead mingled with the wreckage. In all, 1198 people had lost their lives.

Among the 761 fortunate ones were Dr. Foss and Captain Turner. Foss drifted for two hours and was picked up by the tug, *Indian Empire*. After reaching the deck, he collapsed through the shock and exposure. Captain Turner lived to captain again.

The sinking of the *Lusitania* was a temporary military success for the Germans, and the crew received an ovation when it returned to port. Notwithstanding, the outrage at the loss of civilian lives turned into a long-term public relations disaster. The United States didn't care if the German empire had warned them not to travel into the war zone. They viewed this element of total war as barbaric and unjustified. The *New York Times* dedicated six pages to the description of the tragedy. The press used words like "wholesale murder," "piracy," and "slaughter." Leaders like Theodore Roosevelt demanded retribution. President Wilson reluctantly agreed that Germany had crossed a line. Overriding his pacifist Secretary of State and key political ally, William Jennings Bryan, Wilson issued several notes to the German government. Wilson's official statements asserted, "Whatever be the other

---

6. "The Sinking of the *Lusitania*, 1915," Eye Witness to History, www. eyewitnesstohistory.com (2000).

facts regarding the *Lusitania*, the principal fact is that a great steamer, primarily and chiefly a conveyance for passengers, and carrying more than a thousand souls who had no part or lot in the conduct of the war, was torpedoed and sunk without so much as a challenge or a warning, and that men, women, and children were sent to their death in circumstances unparalleled in modern warfare."[7]

While the Germans disagreed who was to blame for the tragedy, they could not afford to add the United States to their list of enemies. By August of 1915, the Germans agreed to restrictions on submarine warfare. They even withdrew all U-boats from the English Channel. For the next several months, they settled for less provocative ways to win a total-war. The crisis averted, Wilson again shifted his attention to domestic issues, and to the chaos south of the border.

Before dawn one spring morning in 1916, the quiet border village of Columbus, New Mexico, was awakened by screams and gunfire. The raid by General Francisco "Pancho" Villa and hundreds of his "Villistas" caught both the town and the nearby army camp totally by surprise. As the Villistas attacked the business district, the citizens of the town fled to the desert or took cover in one of the town's larger buildings. Amid the chaos and fire, the nearby 13th Cavalry rallied its men and set up two Bene-Mercier machine guns to make a stand. The first machine gun, set up in front of the Hoover Hotel, opened up on the bandits, pushing them back and behind cover. The second, set up on East Boundary Street, fired north and caught dozens of Villistas in a deadly crossfire. After an hour and a half, the Villistas slipped away to the South. The body

---

7. Ray Stannard Baker, *Woodrow Wilson: Life and Letters, Neutrality 1914-1915* (New York: Charles Scribner's Sons, 1937), 353.

count revealed approximately seventy-five Villistas and two dozen Americans, including ten civilians.[8]

President Wilson waited a few short weeks for the impotent Mexican government to deal with Villa. Not satisfied with their progress, he federalized the National Guard and sent them to guard the southern border of the United States. The terrifying raids that materialized out of the night had become more regular and appeared to the governor of Texas more and more like deliberate incursions by an organized force. Young Roy Blanchard, a recent inductee of the National Guard, found himself sitting among a large group of young men listening to his commanding officers explain why they were leaving home and traveling by train to the Texas border. The government of Mexico could not control the bandits in Northern Mexico, and therefore the National Guard was needed. While Roy's commanding officer's explanation was simple enough, the reasons why Pancho Villa decided to launch attacks on the United States was decidedly more complicated.

Raids over the border into Texas weren't the first sign of trouble in Mexico. The civil war in Mexico preoccupied Woodrow Wilson from the first days of his presidency. In February 1912, Francisco Madero, elected President of Mexico, was murdered and replaced by General Victoriano Huerta. Wilson refused to recognize a government that gained power through "thuggery" and bided his time waiting for a credible Mexican opposition to form.[9] Meanwhile, Wilson advised all Americans to leave Mexico and forbade anyone to furnish arms to any faction in the ensuing

---

8. http://www.history.army.mil/html/reference/army_flag/mexex.html, accessed August 14, 2013.

9. Frederick S. Calhoun, *Power and Principle: Armed Intervention in Wilsonian Foreign Policy* (Kent: Kent State University Press, 1986), 39–41.

civil war. Wilson's patience didn't prove to be enough of a policy, and in April of 1914, he ordered the seizure of the key Atlantic Mexican port of Veracruz to prevent foreign armaments getting to the Huerta government. The Veracruz occupation successfully weakened Huerta, and helped lead to his abdication in July, 1914. Regretfully, the chaos in Mexico and the instability on the border didn't improve. After a period of waiting for a legitimate leader of Mexico to emerge, President Wilson identified Venustiano Carranza as Mexico's best hope and granted US financial and military support. This did not please Carranza's rivals, most notably Pancho Villa, the capable and charismatic leader of the *División del Norte*.

Facing an unacceptable decline in both power and prestige, Villa chose decisive action as his best path to renewed popularity. Coldly, he calculated that an attack on the unpopular US would rally Mexico behind him. Thus, the border terror began. What started with seemingly random attacks across the border in mid-1915 morphed into regular raids into Texas by fall. Exasperated, the Governor of Texas asked President Wilson for help, but the help would come too late for many.

In January 1916, Villa's men captured and executed seventeen American mining engineers working in Northern Mexico. Two months later, hundreds[10] more raided the town of Columbus, New Mexico.[11] Villa's attacks indeed rallied a large group of people, but not those he'd intended. After vainly waiting a few months for Mexico to apprehend Villa and secure the border, Wilson

---

10. This number is an estimate and various accounts list anything from 500 to 1500.

11. Cooper, *Pivotal Decades*, 227. Heckscher, *Woodrow Wilson*, 387–388.

reluctantly ordered General John J. Pershing to pursue Villa and end his reign of terror.

As Wilson sent Pershing to pursue Villa, he ordered the only remaining military force at his disposal, the National Guard, to protect against further raids across the border. Among those who responded was Roy's Michigan National Guard. In order to accomplish their goal, they had been federalized, combined with the Wisconsin National Guard, and renamed the 32nd Infantry Division.

The National Guard that showed up at the southern border of the US didn't intimidate many. Most of the National Guard units sent to the border were undermanned, under-equipped, and under-trained. To add to this fiasco, many National Guard were in a foul mood. They resented the recent federal seizure of the Guard. Some of the men that Roy served with even refused to take a federal oath or resisted a mobilization at all, on the grounds that they were sworn only to protect their state.[12] Time on the border didn't improve morale. The more evident it became that they would not be part of the active pursuit of Villa in Mexico, and the more time they spent training under the arrogant regular army troops, the more eager the Guard units were to go home. Apparently, the lofty promises made by Guard recruiters at enlistment were not standing up to tough reality. Secretary of War Newton Baker, aware of the morale problems, released some to return to school in the fall, but ended the practice once it became evident that it would cripple the force.[13] But, not everyone clamored to go home; Roy was having a fantastic time.

His fellow guardsmen became a family of sorts. The officers

---

12. Ibid., 156–157.
13. Ibid., 159–163.

he served under became mentors who filled some of the void his father had created by leaving years before. He even developed pride in his own country. The chaos of Mexico across the border gave him increased contentment in his own relatively stable US.

His skills steadily increased. He learned how to fire a rifle and handgun, throw a grenade, and dig an effective trench. The rigors of Army training with the constant drilling and exercise had demonstrably increased his strength, confidence, and self-esteem. Roy also experienced enough occasional adventure to give him something to write home about. Like the incident two miles from Fort Hancock on September 1, 1916.

Fort Hancock wasn't much of a fort. It consisted of fifteen tents with a small barricade around it and trenches in front. Near the trenches ran three sets of railroad tracks. Trains ran through constantly, one rolling through every fifteen or twenty minutes in the days following the Guard's arrival. The town of Hancock was even less impressive, it consisted of a train station, small store and bar, and six dusty adobe huts. Roy was assigned to guard duty every other day. On September 1, Roy's commander assigned him and three other guardsmen to guard a border station two miles from Fort Hancock.

At 10:00 p.m., two cavalry river guards led the four guardsmen across the desert. Their guard station turned out to be not much of a station. Rather, it was an old rickety not-so-secure pump house. From their vantage point in the pump house, they looked over the wide river a mere hundred feet away. As they looked out the window, they imagined bandits, like the ones who decimated Columbus, at every sound. Having three armed companions was some comfort for Roy, but if Villa's bandits crossed the river at their checkpoint, there was precious little they could do.

At around 2:00 a.m., Roy was startled by noises in the bushes nearby. He strained his ears and looked for any reflection off metal or sound of a horse or perhaps whispers in Spanish. He elbowed a fellow guard, and when the bushes rattled again, he squeaked out, "Halt." Disgusted he said, "Halt," again, this time louder and with more authority. The noise in the bushes grew louder, so he did what any teen would do at 2:00 a.m. while guarding the border against raiding bandits: he pulled out his sidearm and starting firing. The noise was deafening in the small pump house, and his other guardsmen tried to grab their weapons and shield their ears at the same time. No bandits fired back, but a wounded coyote did tear out of the bushes, howling, and was subsequently torn to pieces by a pack of eighteen to twenty other hungry coyotes. After the tension of the moment dissipated, Roy and the other guardsmen laughed it off. While the incident wasn't as momentous as fighting off real bandits, it made a good story, and Roy endured teasing about it for months.

The coyotes, ranging in size from twenty-five to forty pounds, ran with their tails down, and fed on small animals. They were everywhere in West Texas, but other than rattling the nerves of greenhorn guardsmen, the nocturnal coyotes were not a threat to humans. Roy bragged to his sister Pearl that they wouldn't harm a man, and dealt with them as a simple annoyance; when he tired of their incessant "yelling" at night, a simple pistol shot in the air drove them off. The deadly rattlers were also a nuisance, as big as four-and-a-half feet long, and everywhere. Roy laughed them off and told Pearl he kept his firearm holstered, merely kicking them out of the way.

His exploits guarding the border from the wildlife weren't the only things worthy of writing home about. He heard tales of a heroic Texas Ranger who disarmed twenty Mexican bandits and marched them three miles back to the fort. He also kept up with the progress of the regular army that was fighting skirmishes with Pancho Villa or small bands of his followers. According to Roy's sources, Pershing had Villa on the run and growing numbers of the Villistas were either in jail or deserting in large numbers. Roy expected to head home in a month or so. Both reports were overly optimistic: Villa continued to evade capture and Roy's last month in Texas kept dragging on month after month until the spring of 1917.

While in Texas, Roy not only learned skills and grew more disciplined amid the rigor of army life, he also witnessed the crudeness of the regular army soldiers. His early excitement for his uniform and camaraderie gave way to wariness, especially after Pearl began to take interest in some of the soldiers that she met back home in Michigan. Feeling protective of his only sister, Roy told Pearl that she could do a lot better, and while he empathized with her being attracted to a man in uniform, he wrote,

> I don't know the fellow you are going with and Pearl I always said I wanted to know the fellow my sister married, before she married him, and you know that you haven't went with him very long. A fellow who has been on the railroad and in the regular army hardly amounts to anything. He might be nice to you but maybe while he is not around you.[14]

Roy offered his services to Pearl as a screen for the soldiers who came courting. He was certain that if he could meet the guy and spend a few minutes with him, then he could tell if he was respectable or a rogue. In the meantime, Roy himself met someone he found respectable. Her name was Mildred Adair, and he fell

---

14. Roy Blanchard, to Pearl Blanchard, 11 November 1916, Roy Blanchard papers, Grand Rapids, MI.

in love with her the moment he saw her. He bravely introduced himself and convinced her to give him her address. Now, he had two people to write to from the border.

Meeting Mildred caused Roy to think again on his financial future. While the National Guard paid better than the odd jobs that he endured in Michigan, the Guard wouldn't pay him enough to help his family and enable him to start one of his own. While his mother's recent marriage had somewhat eased his responsibilities, he still worried. His stepfather was considerably older than his mother and not well off. But worrying about things in the distant future didn't do anyone any good, so Roy shrugged his shoulders and kept positive.

When off duty, he went with his buddies to boxing matches, cheap movies, and whatever else the small town or base put on to keep the men busy. Roy also sat at his bunk writing long letters when the "cold wind full of sand," kept him confined to quarters. "Please write longer letters," he wrote to his sister Pearl. Roy's thoughts turned often to his family in far-away Michigan and a girlfriend whom he hadn't figured out how to provide for yet.

But, seeking his fortune would have to wait. While Roy and the National Guard watched the border, the Army under Pershing had traveled 400 miles south, scattered Villa's irregulars, and killed key leaders, but could not corner Villa himself. With each day that passed, the people and government of Mexico grew more and more impatient with America's armed forces within their borders. With tensions rising in Mexico's government and an untenable situation evolving with Germany, Wilson began to consider calling Pershing back to the United States.

While Americans chased Villa around Northern Mexico, Germany, short on food and desperate to knock out one of the three major powers that it faced, revisited blockading Britain, even at the risk of bringing in powerful neutrals like the US. Their reckless strategy had two parts. First, Germany proposed an alliance with Mexico. If Mexico would attack the United States, Germany would support their efforts to regain the states of Texas, Arizona, and New Mexico. This clumsy and far-fetched proposal via "The Zimmerman Telegram" was intercepted by both the British and US State Department, who were spying on Germany's communications. The second prong of their strategy was to end restrictions on submarine warfare. The German naval staff convinced the Kaiser that their U-boats could sink 600,000 tons of Allied shipping a month. If that held true, the Allies would be at the brink of starvation and would subsequently be unable to continue the war in five months. The Germans believed that, even if their policy changes brought the US into the war, they could starve the Allies before the US could arrive in force.

These decisions poisoned US-German relations and assured that the US would enter the war. When the US public found out that Germany was actively encouraging Mexico to invade the United States, they were outraged. Germany's decision to try to sink any ship that came close to Europe also shocked Americans. Echoing the infamous *Lusitania* tragedy, newspapers soon graphically reported American passengers perishing on neutral vessels sunk by German torpedoes. Next, Germany attacked vessels flying American flags. Neutrality could simply not be maintained any longer. The Atlantic Ocean had once been a vast moat. Now it was a highway of sorts to bring goods to market. The US could not afford to wait for it to become safe again. After months of enduring German subs terrorizing US ships, the US was no longer isolationist. Antiwar parties split, prominent Socialists came out in support of the war, and even the *American Union Against Militarism* fell apart.[15] With no other options left, Wilson reluctantly broke off diplomatic relations with Germany on February 3, 1917, and stoically asked Congress for a declaration of war on April 6, 1917.

Germany's strategies in diplomacy and brutality in the Atlantic reverberated all the way into Mexico for men like Roy. Facing a likely crisis with Germany, and able to take some comfort in the fact that Pershing had scattered Villa's band across the Mexican state of Chihuahua, Wilson ordered the withdrawal of most of the Army from Mexico. Despite the failure of catching Villa, Wilson and his Generals realized that this time chasing Villa and guarding the border had increased the effectiveness of both the regular army and the National Guard. They prayed that those lessons would prove helpful in the hellish trenches of the stalemated Western Front.

---

15. Nell Irvin Painter, *Standing at Armageddon: The United States 1877-1919* (New York: W. W. Norton, 1987), 322.

CHAPTER 4

★ ★ ★ ★ ★

OVER THERE

The World must be made safe for Democracy.
—President Woodrow Wilson

Over there, over there,
Send the word, send the word over there
That the Yanks are coming, the Yanks are coming
The drums rum-tumming everywhere.
So prepare, say a prayer,
Send the word, send the word to beware—
We'll be over, we're coming over,
And we won't come back till it's over, over there.
—Songwriter, George M. Cohen

IN THE DAYS after Congress declared war against the German Empire, volunteers lined up outside recruitment stations across the country. In fact, so many lined up to volunteer for the American Expeditionary Force (AEF) that the government had to institute a draft to keep things orderly.

Wilson chose General John J. "Black Jack" Pershing of Missouri to command the AEF. Pershing, a veteran of numerous campaigns including the Spanish-American War, gained the nickname "Black Jack" by commanding the well-trained and effective Negro 10th Cavalry. Cold, thoughtful, aloof, but fair, Pershing won the respect of common soldiers and presidents alike. His aloofness increased in 1915 after his wife and three out of four children were killed in a tragic fire in San Francisco, but he was still the obvious choice to lead both the punitive expedition into Mexico after Pancho Villa's invasion, and the AEF. While he was unsuccessful in capturing Villa, he did not disappoint in Europe.

As Roy began to train for the war in Europe, President Wilson and his advisors navigated the many decisions before them regarding entering the war and, God-willing, the peace that would follow. Britain, France, and Russia all requested assistance, and Wilson's advisors predicted that, without quick American military and financial support, France and Britain would surely collapse under the weight of the next German offensive. General John Pershing sailed to Europe in May 1917 and quickly determined that America needed to train one million soldiers in the next year.

He also decided that they would be the most help to the Allied cause on the stalemated Western Front.[1]

The location of American entry thus determined, the next question was the manner of organization. Wilson pressed for a single war council to conduct the war in a unified manner; the Allies accepted the proposal in November of 1917. The Supreme War Council provided the general direction for the common war effort but left the specifics up to the individual nations.[2] The United States also chose to keep the American Army in one piece rather than divide and mix it with the French and British troops. They believed that American forces could demonstrate their ability better if they acted independent of Allied forces, and Wilson and Pershing recognized the political reality that America would have a stronger voice at the peace table if America's men fought independently of the British and French.[3]

The men who would make up this uniquely American force came from a wide variety of classes, races, and places of birth. Even those recently off the boat from Europe were caught up in the moment and joined up to become one of Pershing's crusaders. The force that Wilson proposed to send to France consisted of those already in the military, volunteers, and draftees. The educated elite signed up immediately. The chance for adventure appealed to so many college students that it forced Ivy League schools like Princeton to take deliberate steps to ensure that a majority of their

------

1. Calhoun, *Power and Principle*, 176. Other possibilities would have been giving direct assistance to Russia or attacking Germany and opening another front through Turkey.
2. Ibid., 178.
3. Ibid., 179.

undergraduates did not flock to the recruiting stations.[4] Former President Theodore Roosevelt, hoping to relive the adventure of his Rough Rider days, offered to lead a regiment of volunteers chosen from elite schools and men from the West. Appearing hat in hand before President Wilson, Roosevelt explained the benefits of his plan. He proposed that descendants of Civil War generals be included in the leadership as well as French commanders to pay respect to the memory of Lafayette. Wilson listened respectfully to Roosevelt's ideas but firmly declined the offer. Roosevelt's health was declining, and the plan held little real military value.[5]

Roosevelt and his new class of Rough Riders were not the only men clamoring to join the AEF. Volunteer William Langer had his own reasons for enlisting:

> Perhaps we were offended by the arrogance of the German U-boat campaign and convinced that Kaiserism must be smashed, once and for all. Possibly we already felt that, in the American interest, Western democracy must not be allowed to go under. But I doubt it. I can hardly remember a single instance of serious discussion of American policy or of larger war issues. We men, most of us young, were simply fascinated by the prospect of adventure and heroism. Most of us, I think, had the feeling that life, if we survived, would run in the familiar, routine channels. Here was our one great chance for excitement and risk. We could not afford to pass it up.[6]

---

4. David M. Kennedy, *Over Here: The First World War and American Society* (Oxford: Oxford University Press, 1980), 147.

5. Ibid., 148–9.

6. William Langer, *Gas and Flame in World War I* (New York: Knopf, 1965), xviii-xix. Quoted in James H. Hallas, *Doughboy War: The American Expeditionary Force in World War I* (Boulder: Lynne Rienner, 2000), 9.

The lure of seeing exotic places and of becoming a hero like one reads about in adventure stories compelled many to join the armed forces. Dan Edwards, in the Army reserve, knew he would be called to service but decided not to wait and reenlisted on the day that war was declared on Germany. All of Edward's co-workers came with him, and he noted that, "Half of them barely knew where the war was and didn't give a damn."[7] Tony Monaco had only recently come off the boat from Italy but hurried up to the enlistment station and told the clerk, "Ma name Tony Monaco. In dees contra seex months. Gimmie da gun."[8] The enthusiastic recruits reminded many observers of schoolboys on the eve of a big game. They wanted to "see the show," with their own eyes.[9]

The spirit and attitude of the volunteers masked the seriousness of war. The volunteers told jokes, made light of the conflict, and gave nicknames to everything. This disguised their thoughtful reflections, however, about both the conflict and their thoughts about life in general. In serious moments of reflection, they were deeply outraged over both Germany's treatment of civilians in neutral and Allied countries. Their youthful strength and confidence convinced them they could help stop this global bully. While most of them felt invincible, they still calmly wrote where their forbidden diary should be sent should they "cash in" or get "knocked off."

Roy, disgusted with the bully Germans himself, began to

---

7. Hallas, *Doughboy War*, 7.

8. Daniel J. Sweeney, ed., *History of Buffalo and Erie County 1914-1919* (Buffalo, NY: Committee of One Hundred, 1919), 76. Quoted in Hallas, *Doughboy War*, 12.

9. Kennedy, *Over Here*, 185.

keep his own diary. They were officially prohibited because of the real dangers of revealing useful information to the Germans if they were captured. Anyway, Roy ignored the order and began to enter his thoughts and experiences into a diary for the first and last time in his life. It was simply a record of his short observations and rough sketches during the most intense years of his life.[10]

Like other volunteers, Roy believed this was his one chance to see the world and to do something of consequence. When he joined in February 1916, he was only a month over seventeen. When he was discharged on May 20, 1919, he was twenty. He grew two inches (from 5' 6" to 5' 8"), gained weight, learned French, and gained a variety of skills. His general confidence increased as the Army taught him how to fire rifles, manage machine guns, throw grenades, dig trenches, and survive a gas attack. Ultimately, though, his courage would be truly tested when he was ordered to go over the top, straight into battlefields crisscrossed by machine guns and pockmarked by enemy artillery.

The average member of the AEF was 5'7½" tall and 141½ pounds. Roy was almost precisely that size when he joined the National Guard.[11] Most volunteers did not have any prior military service. Thirty-one percent were illiterate and eighteen percent were foreign born.[12]

While the enthusiasm for the war effort encouraged Pershing and Wilson, they quickly reconsidered a volunteer force. The

---

10. David D. Lee, *Sergeant York*, 23. David Kennedy also makes note of this in *Over Here*, 205. Many soldiers were ordered not to keep diaries, but did so anyway.

11. Hallas, *Doughboy War*, 20.

12. Ibid., 11.

prevailing wisdom was that the American way to wage war was through volunteering, but after consideration, Wilson quickly assessed that approach as a sure path to chaos, and realized that excessive volunteering from men working in key industries would actually hamper the country's ability to prosecute the war. Therefore, he pushed for "Selective Service" that would successfully organize the assignment of labor and disturb industry and social structure as little as possible. A draft then, Wilson believed, was appropriate for a country that had already volunteered in mass.[13]

The course set by Wilson and approved by Congress now moved forward to execution with a considerable amount of anxiety. The Civil War, a mere fifty years in the past, still influenced their thinking. The last time the US attempted a draft, the American public responded with the rioting and killing of over 100 draft agents. By the end of the Civil War, the draft had only provided about six percent of the men who fought for the North at an immense social cost. Furthermore, this was a different war fought against a foreign and aggressive foe. Instead of riots, the American public responded with great enthusiasm. On June 5, 1917, ten million men presented themselves at 5,000 local offices with no major incidents. Three days later, a blindfolded Secretary Newton Baker drew the first number out a large glass bowl. The order of call now established the local officials called up those selected for military service. By September, the camps began to receive the first draftees. By war's end, seventy-seven percent of American soldiers in France had joined through the selective service.[14]

---

13. Patterson, *Over Here,* 145–150.

14. Ibid., 145–150.

The War Department now went to work organizing the draftees and volunteers into cohesive divisions. On July 18, 1917, Roy and his fellow National Guard troops from Michigan and Wisconsin officially became the 32nd division of the US military. Joining all of the troops that had been guarding the border from attacks by Pancho Villa were a large number of inexperienced troops who enlisted after the US declaration of war. All gathered at Camp MacArthur in Texas and began training under instructors familiar with the war in France.

Roy came by train to Camp MacArthur. It was vast. The camp covered over thirteen hundred acres on a ten-thousand-acre-plus reservation outside of Waco. The Army put the camp in order quickly. They immediately cleared out the red-light district and built a base hospital, administrative offices, and a tent camp. The 32nd Division formed two brigades. Roy's Michigan infantry formed the 63rd and the Wisconsin infantry formed the 64th. Under the 63rd formed two infantry regiments and one machine-gun battalion. The Army placed Roy in Company K under the 12th Infantry Regiment.[15]

Roy and the other eighteen thousand troops began to train immediately. The officers and non-commissioned officers first received training in infantry specialties. Roy, a non-commissioned officer, eagerly embraced this training: first learning the various new weapons from the Western Front and then instructing the new recruits. In addition to the American officers, walking around the bustling camp were French and British officers who lectured the wide-eyed teenagers about the conditions in the trenches on

15. Joint War History Commissions of Michigan and Wisconsin, *The 32nd Division in the World War: 1919* (Madison: Wisconsin War History Commission, 1920), 27.

the Western Front. The foreign officers told stories of the terrible battles of Ypres, the Somme, and Verdun. Roy listened with awe and foreboding to the danger from unseen enemies firing shell after shell, the muddy lines of trenches, the heroic acts of men disregarding their own safety to rescue wounded comrades.[16] With new energy and resolve, Roy scaled walls, threw grenades, navigated barbed wire, and learned how to dig in under fire. Throughout the training, the weather remained sunny and warm, a far cry from the rain and mud that would become their almost constant companion in France.

By December of 1917, the War Department determined that the 32nd was as ready as any division for service in France. Roy, facing an unknown amount of time in Europe, asked for and was granted a short furlough to see family before leaving Texas. This unusual grace enabled Roy to introduce a few of his new soldier friends to his mother and sister. Unlike his deployment to the Mexican border, this trip was more ominous. While Roy kept up his youthful optimism, Roy's mom and sister bravely fought back the tears as they urged him to stay safe. The time at home was short, however; on January 2, 1918, the first excited troops left Waco, and by March 1, the vast majority had made the long train ride to Hoboken, New Jersey—their port of embarkation.[17]

Roy had left the American Midwest far behind. He wondered if he would ever see it again.

---

16. Ibid., 30.
17. Ibid., 32.

*Corporal Roy Blanchard before leaving
the United States for France*

Camp Merritt, located near the suburban town of Dumont, New Jersey, and about fifteen miles from Times Square, New York City, became the 126th's home for three weeks. Roy appreciated the accommodations and put up with the food and the zero-degree weather. Too cold to drill and train, the soldiers hiked to stay in top condition. Up early, Roy slid out from warm covers, put on his uniform and slogged through six to ten mile hikes down the local ice and snow covered roads. As they marched in unison down old roads and snow covered hills, they talked of General Washington and cold Valley Forge. In the afternoons, they kept their equipment in tip-top shape and listened to lectures on military tactics and how to talk with French locals. The officers of the 126th later noted that the soldiers learned French much better once they had to know it to "parley with the mademoiselles in France," but nonetheless they made an effort.[18] Measles, scarlet fever, and mumps made their rounds among the close quarters, and many men were quarantined in their barracks. Being inside wasn't all bad; the YMCA did their best to entertain men in the camp, but many missed opportunities to see New York City. Healthy or not, the officers were stingy with the weekend passes. Luckily, Roy managed to secure one, and joined the train loads of teenage soldiers gaping at dazzling New York City. In awe of all the lights and with senses sharpened by the impending cross-Atlantic adventure, Roy wrote to Pearl,

I feel quite comical to-night Eat, drink and be merry, for on the morrow we--------have to hike another fifteen or twenty miles.

You ought to have been to the Midnight Follies with me here in New York.

Everything was millionaire, from the check maid to the leading lady. We did not make a hit, simply because I have all the girl I want right at home . . .

New York is some burg just the same. We were in the swellest cabaret on the Bowery and bought cigars in the Astoria Hotel.

We lamped the city from the sky point of the Woolworth Bldg. That building sways nearly a foot.

Tell Ma, I got the gloves and wristlets and thank her very much for them.

---

18. Emil B. Gansser, *History of the 126th Infantry in the War with Germany* (Grand Rapids: 126th Infantry Association, 1920), 38.

I have heavy sox enough now, in fact I am all set for anything that might come.

... The police (except the females) are polite to women and soldiers but they are bull dogs to men. One fellow fell down in the black mud and water and a wagon (light spring) ran over him. He looked like a shade in a heart hand, but the blue pacer told him to "lift his carcass and blow." Of course he did.

... Listen dear, I have an idea this war is not going to last very long. Probably just long enough so we see a good portion of France and maybe a little action in the ditches. ...

Your dear Sammie Brother.

Roy.

The New York that Roy visited towered above the world. The Woolworth building, sixty stories tall (792 feet) and featuring over 5,000 windows, had been completed in 1913. Roy and his soldier friends looked over the city from the observation deck on the 57th floor. The Gothic architecture and the ornate lobby wowed the young men from Michigan and Wisconsin.[19] The seventeen-story, twenty-year-old Waldorf/Astoria hotel also wowed Roy with its high ceilings, beautiful statues, and giant fireplace. Coney Island and Brighton Beach did their best to attract soldiers looking to blow off steam before they left for the war; the soldiers could pick from dancing, Broadway Revue, Cabaret, seaside walks, southern Jazz Bands, intriguing restaurants, billiards, fishing, handball, or tennis. Not surprisingly, these groups of training, hiking, and touring teens developed nicknames. Sammies was the name given

---

19. http://en.wikipedia.org/wiki/Woolworth_Building, accessed September 9, 2014.

to the Americans by the English—a play on Uncle Sam. This name did not really take hold, however, and most soldiers referred to themselves as "Yanks" or "Doughboys."[20] The origin of the name "Doughboy" is hard to determine, but was perhaps given to the army that had chased Villa on long marches covered with adobe dust. "Adobies" is easily shortened to "dobies," and then changed to "doughboys."[21] Once in France, Roy referred to himself and his comrades as Yanks.

Whatever their nickname, the American soldiers trained and waited for their time to cross the Atlantic. While they waited, news came that the American transport *Tuscania* had encountered a German submarine eight miles from the Irish coast. The German submarine, U-77 fired two torpedoes, hitting the 14,000 ton steamer in the starboard side. The other ships in the convoy came quickly to its aid, though, and while the *Tuscania* sank, 2,187 of the 2,397 servicemen were rescued. Thirteen of the men who went down with the *Tuscania* were from the 32nd Division, the first casualties of the war for Roy's division, which made the loss all the more disconcerting. Roy's trip across the Atlantic was getting closer, and the sinking of the *Tuscania* worried him.

Starting in Camp Merritt, the soldiers' mail was censored and visitors to camp were few. The men, now knowing others who had been killed by the Germans, were eager to avenge their deaths. While they waited, the army issued men uniforms, gas masks, and weapons. The officers were supplied by their own means, and Roy received everything from thick socks to a .45 caliber pistol from

20. Hallas, *Doughboy War,* 2.

21. Laurence Stallings, *The Doughboys: The Story of the AEF, 1917-1918* (New York: Harper and Row, 1963), 5.

friends and family back home.[22] The gas mask was worrisome. It looked strange and made breathing uncomfortable. Made of treated canvas, it had two inset glass eye lenses that made the wearer look like a giant insect. Straps wrapped around the back of the head to keep it in place, and a clip squeezed the nose shut. The wearer breathed exclusively through the mouth using a cloth-covered tube that was attached to a small metal box containing activated charcoal. The British had developed the device and proved its effectiveness for surviving certain types of gas attacks. Roy was glad to have it but dreaded putting it on. Officers were ordered to pack useless items as well—such as white collars and cuffs for important occasions in France. When they arrived, those orders were countermanded and this useless equipment was packed away and stored, in many cases never to be seen again.[23]

On February 10, the army ordered the 126th to complete applications for war risk insurance, prepare sailing lists, and to pack barrack bags. On February 15, an advanced set of officers boarded the ship. On February 16, the regiment marched from camp to Dumont and took a train to Hoboken where Roy and his sharply uniformed Yank brethren marched through the principal streets of the bustling city.

Smirking at the irony, Officers noted that the inhabitants of Hoboken were primarily from Germany, and that the ship they were about to board had been confiscated from the Hamburg-American Steamship Company, a German corporation. Roy and the 126th had a short wait before boarding the ship, but the Red

---

22. One of the ironies with Roy's experience overseas is that pistol is only referenced once. While in France, a friend stole it, emptied it into the air and ground in a drunken fit of revelry one night in a small French town.
23. Gansser, *History of the 126th*, 38.

Cross ladies made the best of the situation serving the men hot coffee and pastries. By mid-afternoon, it was Roy's turn. With his heavy pack on his small frame, he walked in line toward the large troopship *President Grant*. His friends joked and waved to the onlookers saying their goodbyes to America. The gangplank swayed as they clomped aboard. Roy looked forward at the ship and thought briefly about German submarines but then pushed back the fear, smiled, and looked back at the waving well-wishers. He waved as he stepped onto the ship. It would be a long year until he stepped on American soil again. By 3:00 p.m., all 2,836 enlisted men and 99 officers had boarded the *President Grant* via gangplank and received the number of their berth.[24] Their time in dazzling New York and frigid New Jersey was over.

Roy boarded the ship with friends from home and officers he knew. Men in his regiment received mention in his local newspaper and appeared in letters from his family. While the ship and the experience were unfamiliar, his fellow soldiers were not. With these friends, Roy spent the day promenading the decks of the *President Grant,* pointing and chatting about the imposing New York skyline and the busy shipping in the harbor. They spent the night in bunks, stacked three high and squeezed in every available space on the two decks below the main deck. In the morning, they saw a steady stream of ferry boats steam by, crowded with passengers waving and bidding them farewell. Finally, by mid afternoon, a small tug pulled them out into the center of the Hudson River.

Getting overseas proved slow for Roy, but he enjoyed the sights and experiences along the way. Several miles from shore, the

---

24. Members of the 107th, 509th engineers, Service Battalion, and members of the Headquarters Detachment filled in all the empty spots on the ship. The total aboard numbered 5,300. Gansser, *History of the 126th*, 39–40.

ship dropped anchor next to several other transports and one US cruiser. Creative artists had painted the ships in every conceivable camouflage pattern, hoping to make them difficult for submarines to see them against the sky and waves. The next morning, the soldiers strained their eyes for the Statue of Liberty, faint through the mist, their final connection to home. Before midnight, the convoy weighed anchor and moved out to sea, passing into international waters after midnight. It was February 19, 1918, and Roy's foreign service had begun.

The sea was rough the first days out: pitching back and forth, making life miserable for many. More of a worry though was the German submarine threat. To prepare for the worst-case scenario, the officers led them in the "abandon ship drill" fifteen minutes before every dawn and at dusk. Each man was issued a life belt, ordered to be worn any time they were away from their bunk. Each man was assigned to a life boat. When the siren rang, men assembled at their life boat, if they were one of the lucky ones. Due to the packed nature of the ship, more than half the troops were assigned to rafts. The sergeants of the regiment were assigned to sentry boxes connected to the bridge by telephone. In pairs, the lookouts kept watch on a sector of the ocean for an hour at a time, using a set of field glasses. After years of submarine warfare, crews had discovered that the most dangerous time was the break of day and just before sunset. A sharp eye was critical; the safety of the ship depended upon quick maneuvering as soon as a periscope, or the track of an approaching torpedo was sighted.[25]

Besides safety drills and sharp lookouts, the ship took additional measures. Smoking was forbidden on decks between sunset and sunrise. To make sure the ban was enforced, only officers carried

25. Ibid., 42.

matches. All lights on the ship were extinguished at sunset, unless the light could not be seen from the outside. Precautions now taken, still the men remained anxious. The hulls of the *Lusitania*, the *Tuscania*, and hundreds of other vessels lay at the bottom of the Atlantic at the hands of German U-boat captains. Their wariness was well-founded. Two days out from New York, a German submarine torpedoed a tanker fifty miles ahead of the convoy. The convoy then changed course to avoid the location where the submarine was last seen.

As they headed south toward the Gulf Stream, the weather warmed and the waves lessened. Few ships were seen, and those few had camouflage. On February 23, the transports *George Washington* and the *De Kalb* joined the convoy, making it the largest group of ships that the United States had sent across to that date. In the afternoon, Roy listened to the band the army enlisted to keep the men entertained and, in the evening, Roy laughed along with his buddies at the latest silent pictures in the mess hall accompanied by the band.

On Friday, March 1, while the regimental band was giving a concert, the cruiser guarding the convoy opened fire and blew a whistle. More cannon fire followed, and the shrill shriek of the siren followed. Roy rushed to his appointed "abandon ship drill" location, straining his eyes for any sign of a German U-boat and thinking of the cold water below. A few young soldiers, overcome by fright, fell to their knees and begged God to save them. Other soldiers dragged them to their posts.

The convoy ships scattered, clouds of black smoke pouring from their funnels and all ships' guns aimed at some object in the water, which all assumed was a periscope. As the other ships scattered and the *President Grant* approached the object, it turned out to be a large discarded barrel. While the threat was false, the reaction was textbook. The Navy plan against submarine attack was for each ship to scatter without regard to its sister ships, on the principle that the loss of one ship was better than the loss of several. Roy, on the *President Grant*, was grimly reminded by those in the know that they were the slowest ship in the convoy.

As they approached Europe, the danger increased. The convoy was met by a destroyer fleet which encircled it to protect the troops from the submarine threat. The cruiser *Huntington*, now superfluous, headed back to the United States. From this point on, the convoy took an additional precaution. To make the ships harder to hit by torpedo, they zigzagged back and forth in formation, all the while protected by the fast-moving, fearsome-looking destroyers.

At the "abandon ship drill," early the next morning, mist encircled the fleet and the men gazed down into the black water, silently wishing that they would have no occasion to get in their life rafts. With each mile, they got closer to dry land, but also in the forefront of their mind was the fact that the waters they were entering had the greatest concentration of German submarines on their voyage. The Germans knew that every soldier they prevented from reaching France was one they didn't have to fight on the Western Front. Finally, whether it was the zigzag course taken by the convoy, or the luck of being in the right place at the right time, Roy's convoy made it safely to their port in Brest. As they pulled into harbor, they watched hydroplanes and a dirigible circling the harbor, keeping an eye out for submarines. While waiting to disembark, the men were entertained by the YMCA and amused by French girls who rowed out near the ship and asked the soldiers to toss them pennies or cigarettes that they caught in their aprons.

After docking at Brest, the 126th disembarked. With relief, Roy put on his heavy pack and walked across the gangplank to French soil. He smiled at surviving the passage across the Atlantic and began to take in the sights and sounds of the French coast. His commanding officers, however, reminded the soldiers quickly that they were not there as tourists. On shore, the 126th moved inland and took up temporary work with the Service of Supply. While digging ditches and working on infrastructure didn't appeal to the 126th, the teenage soldiers still found plenty to laugh at. The French trains, with four wheels for each car, seemed like toys to the young men used to the much bigger Pullmans. One young man from Michigan made a loud show of searching for a key to wind up the miniature train. The officers rolled their eyes at the hijinks and watched the troops who already were looking for shiny French souvenirs.[26]

From Brest, Roy and his regiment traveled south to St. Nazaire, alternating between picturesque French countryside and then going past giant factories where war munitions were being manufactured. The factory workers, primarily French women, came out to cheer the American soldiers at each stop.

The warm spring weather lightened Roy's mood. New crops were springing up, fruit was appearing on the trees, and the clustered towns and villages surrounded by open fields were a distinct contrast to the isolated farm houses that dotted the landscape back home. The 126th arrived at St. Nazaire between March 7 and 8, stiff and sore from the long train ride. After gathering their things, Roy and his regiment marched four miles to their camp.[27]

The camp, established by the French, was floorless, wooden, and leaky. The Americans quickly organized around the clock efforts to prepare the camp for the coming flood of American soldiers. Other than Sundays, the men worked in day and night shifts

26. Ibid., 48.
27. Ibid., 49–51.

unloading transports, building roads, constructing railroad yards, and improving dock facilities.

On March 11, Roy and a detail of one hundred men took a break from camp building to guard a supply shipment. They visited La Valdahon, a scenic town near the Switzerland border. France was interesting and bright and cheery in this sector. Other than the lack of French men of military age in the towns, there was no sign of the desperate battles taking place on the Western Front. Roy spent his free time studying French, aided by his army-issued pocket French dictionary.[28] The chief problem that Roy ran into was that the occupants of the small towns he visited didn't understand his carefully practiced French phrases with his Grand Rapids accent. He laughed it off and wrote Pearl that the French "didn't appear to speak their own language."[29] Despite the language barrier, his fellow soldiers were already falling for the exotic French girls that lined the streets to welcome the American soldiers. Roy also delighted in the funny outfits the French children wore—little straight pants that ended at the knees with short socks and wooden shoes. He wrote to Pearl about all of these things, reminded her that he was still loyal to Mildred, and always begged her to write longer letters.

When he wasn't writing to Pearl, he wrote often in his forbidden diary. He labeled the first page, "keep out," and wrote instructions where to send the diary and pictures of his sister in case of his

---

28. Hallas, *Doughboy War,* 49.

29. Joint War History Commissions of Michigan and Wisconsin, *The 32nd Division in the World War,* 37. Clark Blanchard, son of Roy Blanchard, interview by the author, 4 August 2000. Despite his difficulties, Blanchard stuck with it, writing French phrases to his sister and practicing in his diary. Whether they were useful or not, speaking short French phrases became one of the enduring influences from his time in the war.

death. He also used the diary to keep track of men under his care in accordance with his position of Corporal of the Guard. The Corporal of the Guard was responsible for posting and relieving sentinels and instructing the members of his relief concerning their orders and duties.[30] These lists were kept in his diary with times of guard duty for each soldier in relief. He also chronicled the things he saw—horses, soldiers with different hats and helmets, chickens, dogs, as well as troop positions and diagrams of dugouts and different weapons.

Not everything Roy saw and heard in his early days in France was pleasant to record. Hoping to show the soldiers why they were fighting and whom they were fighting against, the US government shared with their soldiers exaggerated reports handed to them by the British. The reports were horrific, but Blanchard wrote them down the best he could.

Of the many outrages committed by the Boche. Shooting down 500 innocent civilian at Menden. Cutting wounded amex soldiers necks. Castrating non-combatant Red Cross men at Clauseau. Raping of 27 young girls in St. La Aines Cutting women's breasts. Burning children's feet, tongue and eyes.

Hanging men fit for French army. Raping woman who is about to give birth to child. Next day child is born. Child ruthlessly slaughtered before mothers eyes.

Woman's abdomen slashed from womb to breast. Massacre at Belleongonza.

Thousand are killed in village square and burned. Village of

---

30. William H. Waldron, *The Infantry Soldier's Handbook* (New York: Lyons, 2000), 222.

Marque burned, inhabitants shot, burned, murdered and woman raped. Separation of male sex from female sex at Liur. Men made to dig graves for themselves. Girls between 18 and 26 raped to death. Little girl runs around street crazy. Caused by repeated rape.[31]

The reports, circulated among the American infantry, were taken at face value. Exaggerated or not, the reports hardened the teenage soldiers' resolve.[32] America didn't start the war, didn't appreciate unrestricted submarine warfare, and had gradually come to see the German Empire as an international bully.

Roy wasn't aware of it, but Germany was plotting to make his landing irrelevant. Germany was determined to end the war before the Americans could mount an effective defense of France. As Roy was training for his time in the trenches, and as the Americans began landing in France by the thousands, the German Empire was preparing a series of massive assaults. The Germans knew that they needed to strike quickly and decisively to obliterate the British, overrun the French, and force the Americans back into the Atlantic. The plan called for an abrupt and lethal beginning, five hours of shelling from seven thousand German artillery pieces aimed at a weak British sector of the lines.

31. Roy Blanchard, undated diary entry, Roy Blanchard papers, Grand Rapids, MI. His granddaughter was grateful for the warning *Don't read* eighty years later when reading parts of the diary to her children.

32. The Bryce report was put together by the British in 1915 and the report details some of the same stories of German atrocities found in Blanchard's diary. Francis Whiting Halsey, *The Literary Digest History of the World War,* 1 (New York: Funk and Wagnalls, 1919), 361.

CHAPTER 5

★ ★ ★ ★ ★

HOLD THE LINE

*First a shell blew one door in and then the other near me.
The candles went out, and we groped for our gas-helmets in
the dark. Splinters of metal were making sparks as they fell
through just above us, and the din was quite indescribable.
Soon amongst the high-explosive shells falling all around
we heard the unmistakable plop, plop as gas-shells fell
mixed with the others, and the burnt-potato
or onion smell warned us it was time to put
on our gas-helmets.*

*One poor chap couldn't find his helmet; another had his
torn across his face by a flying piece of shrapnel. We waited
apprehensively for a direct hit any moment, but luckily
none came and the barrage lifted back to the front line and
also to the artillery lines. We then all staggered out to find
our battle positions, trying as best we could to see through
helmet eyepieces and the dense fog.*
—British Captain Geoffrey Lawrence,
first day of the 1918 Spring Offensive

──────────── ★ ★ ★ ★ ★ ────────────

W HEN ROY'S 32ND Division arrived in France, the Great War had been grinding on for over three years. Though called the "War to End All Wars," it was the "War that Went on Forever" to those in it. The lines were static, the casualties horrendous, and hope for any breakthrough was fleeting. On the home front, Germany, France, and Britain all rationed food and fuel—in the midst of the coldest winter in 120 years.

Before leaving America, Roy wrote to Pearl telling her that he expected the Americans to defeat the Germans quickly after a little bit of time in the trenches. Reality was something entirely different. Day after day, Roy's commanding officers lectured the exuberant American soldiers about the virtue of caution. Roy's commanding officers knew from news reports and foreign soldiers that the shelling and machine-gun nests on the Western Front were lethal.

By the time the Americans arrived on the continent, the powerful and experienced Allied armies were exhausted. Despite launching massive, carefully planned offensives, despite skilled use of artillery and terrifying new weapons, despite spending the lives of millions of courageous young men, the lines remained frozen from the English Channel to the Swiss border. The regular and sometimes overwhelming use of artillery had turned scenic farmland into a 400-mile-long zone of devastation. Forests had been bombed into muddy wastelands for a mile or two on each side of No Man's Land, and few buildings stood in the immediate area beyond that. In areas that had been the sites of epic engagements, whole villages had been bombed off the map, leaving nothing but brick dust or piles of stones.[1]

The worst of these monumental battles had been 1916's Battle of the Somme. Allied artillery prepared the battle ground by launching over 100,000 shells a day. The shelling was so intense it could be heard sixty to seventy miles away. After five days of intense bombardment, the Allies believed that no living thing could have survived that barrage. But the Germans had survived by retreating underground, beyond where the bombs could penetrate. After the bombardment, the British soldiers crawled up from their trenches and slowly advanced toward the German lines. Some officers kicked soccer balls to show the men where to advance, displaying trademark British calm. As they marched shoulder to shoulder, confident in the work done by their artillery, they walked into a wall of bullets. The Germans had returned to their positions after the shelling lifted, set up machine guns, and mowed down line after line of the slow moving line of khaki-clad soldiers. German soldiers recalled later that it was like knocking over toy soldiers with your finger. On the first day of the Somme, July 1, 1916, the British lost 20,000 soldiers in action with an additional 40,000 wounded, the biggest military disaster in the history of the British Empire. By the end of that day, even some of the German machine gunners were weeping, begging the British to stop their pointless advance.

The British and the French continued on the doomed offensive until November, gaining a mere ten miles of ground and costing the Allies three quarters of a million casualties, including 72,000 missing who had been blown to oblivion or been swallowed by the mud.[2] The British Empire never fully recovered after the Somme.

---

1. Keegan, *The First World War*, 309–310.

2. Keegan, *The First World War*, 286-299. http://www.pbs.org/greatwar/historian/hist_keegan_04_shells.html, accessed July 25, 2015.

France couldn't learn from British mistakes. They endured horrific casualties, retaking Verdun in 1916 and fighting the battle of Arras in early 1917. Convinced that the Western Front was mud, blood, and futility, half the French army gave a list of demands to their commanding officers and simply refused to advance any more.[3]

To make matters worse for the Allies, the Russian Empire, having lost two million soldiers and facing a revolution, gave up in December of 1916. After Germany forced Russia to sign a one-sided peace treaty in March of 1917, they began to transfer its remaining military might to the Western Front.

The hope for the exhausted British and the disillusioned French in the spring of 1918 was the green but enthusiastic AEF that arrived on the continent in convoy after convoy of troop transports through submarine infested waters. While the Allies hurried the American preparations, the Germans moved everyone and everything possible to the Western Front. Everyone possible meant 192 divisions—thirty more than the British and French combined. Even after over three years of war on two fronts, The German Army fielded 3.5 million men. Everything meant massive amounts of artillery brought from the Eastern Front and enough firepower to lay down an earth-shattering bombardment and dissolve the Allied lines.

The French, British, and American generals spent March of 1918 fretting and trying to pinpoint where this offensive might come. Only the German high command knew that answer. The chief strategist for the 1918 German offensive, Erich Ludendorff—a

---

3. Keegan, *The First World War*, 329-330. Fifty-four divisions were involved in this mutiny. They agreed to hold the line against German advances, but they refused to reenter the trenches. Order was not fully restored until August of 1917.

brilliant Prussian general who had achieved fame by destroying the Russians at the Battle of Tannenberg—planned a series of strategic offensives. His primary objective was simple: knock out the British by separating them from the French army on the Somme and driving them back to the English Channel. With Britain out of the war, the French would collapse and the Americans would determine that the war was a lost cause. The specific strategy for this offensive centered on devastating artillery fire, squads of elite and specifically-trained German shock troopers, and rapid momentum.

Ludendorff's strategy worked, initially.

German Artillery on the Western Front

At 4:40 a.m., March 21, 1918, seven thousand German artillery pieces, positioned quietly and hidden by fog, opened up on command. In the space of four hours, the Germans fired a million shells. The barrels of the German cannon glowed red and the thick powder smoke filled the battery positions, making it impossible to even see the next gun over. Soldiers on both sides could not hear anything save the rolling thunder of guns. The earth trembled, twisted, and flew apart. From behind the lines where British artillery was deployed and moving back toward the front, the British lines lost all form. Telephone lines, barbed wire, trenches, and British soldiers were all blown apart and buried by the never-ending barrage of shells. The constant shelling blew doors off the dugouts, extinguished the candles, and sent stunned soldiers stumbling around in the dark for gas masks. The explosive shells were followed by the "plop plop" of gas-shells—an odor similar to burnt potatoes or onions warned the soldiers it was time to put on masks or face a painful and certain death. As soon as the artillery stopped, the British who were able staggered to their battle positions.[4] When they came to the surface from their dugouts, the dazed soldiers recognized nothing. Their elaborate trench systems and block houses had been utterly destroyed. The barbed wire entanglements were broken. Their line could not possibly hold.

The first wave of German soldiers came next. Slipping quietly through the fog, the German infantry encountered little resistance. The British were disheveled and dazed. The telephone lines had been cut, and they had no way to call for artillery support or reinforcements. Their one choice was to surrender.[5] After

4. MacDonald, *To The Last Man*, 82.

5. Ibid., 82–91.

two days, the Germans had advanced fourteen miles, but their reach stretched even further. With them, they hauled a 180-ton cannon by rail—a cannon that could fire a 280-pound shell a distance of seventy-five miles. On March 25, the citizens of Paris screamed and fled as the giant shells began to fall indiscriminately in the streets of Paris. This was the breakthrough Germany had dreamed of and the Allies had feared. German leadership was ecstatic.

As the British and French unified their command and prepared for worst-case scenarios, the Americans resisted panic.[6] Ignoring frantic requests for Americans to be thrown in as untrained replacements, Pershing instead insisted that the American soldiers complete their training. Still, Pershing knew that the Americans needed to get ready and do so quickly.

Roy's 126th got the news soon after the German advance had begun. They hadn't heard the shelling and they hadn't seen the massive German breakthrough, but they heard the messages from official channels and saw it in the frightened eyes of their French hosts. Day after day, news of German progress filtered in. Despite the danger, the Americans were eager to be done with the training and defend their new friends in France. When they finally heard the news that the American troops would indeed be sent to help halt the German advance, they cheered and congratulated each other. Roy joined in the celebration.

Determined, the Americans geared up and set off on trains heading toward the Western Front. They traveled past Nantes, Tours, as well as large aviation training fields. As they rode by, the soldiers gaped and pointed at the pilots performing daring stunts high above their plodding train cars. They also quietly watched

---

6. Eisenhower, *Yanks*, 109–110.

trainloads of wounded French soldiers heading away from the front toward hospitals in southern France, as well as the endless lines of dejected refugees heading away from the front lines.[7] Arriving in Champlitte, the Americans were welcomed warmly by the locals who, despite the battle for existence taking place miles away, took the time to share the history of their ancient town. The American soldiers, most of them away from home for the first time, took notes like tourists.

> At one time the Romans governed the town and built a stout stone wall around it, part of which still stands. Way back in the 16th century, so the inhabitants told us, the Spaniards overran this section and the French peasantry, becoming incensed at their overbearing conduct, drove them out of the country. One building with ten-foot walls of solid stone, still stands, being the only building that withstood the rage of the populace.[8]

Everywhere Roy and the 126th looked there was history. Crumbling castles, ancient hotels frequented by Henry the IV, chateau's dating back to the 16th century, and sites of battles long celebrated by the inhabitants of the town. The citizens enjoyed filling in the teenage soldiers about the importance of their town. Clearly, the French citizens, were more enthusiastic about their past than their future. Many of them expressed pessimism that the American soldiers would do little but extend the suffering of the war. After the humiliating French loss in the Franco-Prussian war, and the four years of futility in the current struggle, they saw the Germans as all but unbeatable.

---

7. Gansser, *History of the 126th*, 53–54.

8. Ibid., 55.

The Americans, intrigued by the ancient curiosities of the town, and undaunted by the pessimism of their French hosts, went about their responsibilities. The 126th spent the next several weeks in an extensive training schedule, which was carried out day after day, rain or shine. Roy and the other soldiers marched two miles each way to the drill fields carrying 100 pound packs. While on the road, they practiced with their gas masks and helmets. The drills included bayonets, attack formations, and learning what the French had to teach them about throwing hand-grenades and using rifle grenades. In addition to the six hours of drills and the hikes to and from the drill fields, the men had the occasional drama. With their packs strapped on their backs as they ran uphill, an officer would yell, "Gas!" and everyone scrambled to put on their masks.

Specific companies had special training with their guns, carts, animals, cannons, signals, or trench mortars, depending on where they were assigned.[9] Roy described it to Pearl, saying,

> We had quite a battle the other night. But it was only a mock raid to give us an idea how it goes. The star shells go up and bust like our 4th of July fireworks. Little parachutes come down and light up all movement under them. The automatic rifles were sure spitting fire, about ten at once were shooting rapid fire. Then the hand and rifle grenades burst and make a boom for each one. It sure was pretty. [10]

As the 32nd Division, including Roy's 126th Regiment, was marveling at the spectacle of mock raids, flares, and automatic rifles, the American 1st Division slipped into the front lines in Picardy, north of Paris. Roy and the other Americans waited eagerly each

9. Ibid., 55–56.
10. Roy Blanchard, Letter to Pearl, May 5, 1918.

day to hear how their fellow doughboys handled the challenges at the front. But, before the 1st could get into the action, Roy's 32nd received their orders to move out. Pershing had determined that the 32nd was ready.

Yanks going into action France

On May 15, 2:30 a.m., trudging along the roads in France, Roy and the thousands that made up the 126th marched thirteen miles through the dark. Roy took his place in the long line of uniformed men arranged four across. As they left camp, Roy turned and waved to their French hosts who lined the roads to bid them goodbye and good luck. The men, encouraged by their new friends, marched along the road singing, excited about heading to the front and getting an opportunity to do what they had been trained to do. The soldiers talked about holding the line against this latest German advance, helping to turn the tide of this war; some even echoed President Wilson and commented about making the world safe for democracy. After the thirteen-mile hike to the train station in a small village, Roy's 126th once again boarded the miniature French trains and headed east.

> The journey took us through a beautiful section of France and as we neared the eastern border, the countryside fairly breathed of historical romance and memories of centuries past. The landscape was a panorama of green meadows and growing crops, and orchards were loaded with fruit. It was a peaceful scene which met our eyes.[11]

All was peaceful and serene, fitting a guided tour of France with their friends. That is, until they reached Belfort. As they pulled up to the station, the bombed-out buildings near the station testified of what was to come.

The 126th got off the train and hiked to their position near Guevenatten. They were now in Alsace, a German province before the war. The 126th thus earned the distinction of being the first American troops to enter Germany. The French had battled over the territory early in the war, but the lines had been static since September, 1914. The city of Belfort, over 3,000 feet above sea level, lies in the pass between the Alps and the Vosges Mountain ranges. Surrounded by fortified hills, it was naturally one of the strongest positions of defense on the French frontier. [12] The city had been gallantly defended in the distant past against fearsome Teutonic tribes and it had been visited by Napoleon as he set off to conquer Germany over 100 years previously. Now, it was to be defended by teenage citizen-soldiers from the Midwest.

On May 19, the company commanders and platoon sergeants from the 126th made a preliminary reconnaissance of the French-

---

11. Gansser, *History of the 126th*, 60–61.
12. Ibid., 61.

controlled trenches. On May 20, Roy checked the contents of his pack: 100 rounds of ammunition, bayonet, pistol, trench knife, first-aid packet, canteen, two blankets, one shelter half, one bed sack, one overcoat, one slicker, two-day reserve rations, toilet articles, entrenching tools, tromblon,[13] helmet, and gas mask.[14] All told, his pack weighed 100 pounds, heavy on his 150 pound frame. Considering his mortality and remembering the bombed out buildings and the rows of injured French soldiers he had seen from the train, Roy wrote in his diary bookmarked by a small silk US flag, "If I should cash in, please put this flag on my cross."

Shouldering their heavy packs, Roy and the 126th marched on a long narrow road heading away from safety and toward the distant artillery. The thousands of soldiers, row upon row, first sang to pass the time; but as the road led them into a small forest, they could hear artillery in the distance—*krump, krump*. Faint staccato machine gun fire echoed—*rat-a-tat-tat*. They switched to single file. The only noise the Americans now made was the steady *crunch, crunch, crunch* of their boots on the gravel path. Flares in the distance and artillery flashes cast eerie shadows through the trees. In time, they marched out of the forest into a cool moonless night. On the eastern outskirts of a quaint village, French guides joined the Americans and led Roy's 126th quietly into the front lines through the maze of support trenches and barbed-wire entanglements.

Following the French guides, the American soldiers stumbled and ran into each other, making slow progress in the unfamiliar dark. They passed signs with arrows, but they were in French and it

---

13. Discharger for a rifle grenade.
14. Blanchard, Diary, undated.

was too dark to clearly make out the words. Finally, they arrived at their positions just before 4:00 a.m. The seven-foot-deep trenches had duck-board walks and ran parallel to the German lines. The French guides briefly explained the layout of the trenches to the Americans, pointing out the zigzagging communication trenches that ran perpendicular out into No Man's Land toward the German positions.

Roy, together with his buddies of Company K, entered and took their position in the reserve trenches. Company I had been chosen to move on further and take the first sector of the front lines. Members of Company I stepped up onto the fire step, eyes wide open, peering over the sandbag parapet. All was quiet, save the shuffling of men in wool uniforms and the whispers back and forth.

The bare trunks of trees and the posts of the barbed wire entanglements looked eerie and surreal in the dark, and the darkness coupled with the uneven ground made it difficult to walk around comfortably and quietly. The trenches were not dug in straight lines. Instead they turned or kinked at angles so that if one part of the trenches was overrun, men with rifles or machine guns could not pin down long stretches of the trench. These trenches were the strength of the front line against Germany, but in order to keep their eyes on enemy activity, the French had dug zigzagging communication trenches out seven hundred yards into No Man's Land. These trenches, 400 to 600 yards apart, ended in a manned observation post about halfway to the German lines. Men at these areas could keep an eye on the enemy and alert the others if the Germans began an advance. Behind the front lines were reserve trenches. These trenches were dug some 200 feet behind the front line and connected with winding communication trenches that enabled reserves to approach the front line without exposing themselves to enemy fire. Roy settled into his spot and looked toward the front lines. He could see how easy it would be to get lost in the maze of trenches and resolved to draw a map as soon as possible.[15]

As daylight broke, Company I of the 126th nervously scanned No Man's Land. In front of their trenches were yards and yards and yards of barbed wire. Roy's comrade, Private Joseph Guyton, looked to the side at the scraped-out recess in the side of the trench where he had laid his pack. Down below and behind the fire step where he stood was the duck-work of the trenches, which were a series of two long boards with slatted boards nailed across them to make a dry pathway through the muddy trenches.

The French taught the Americans how to survive the trenches. On the front lines, there were several responsibilities. First, the troops needed to keep watch. In order to do that, they needed to become familiar with their surroundings. They needed to know the location of the different company and platoon posts of command as well as the day and night observation posts. Those on watch needed to stay alert for raids and gas attacks: ready to fire or relay rocket signals from the front to the back in emergencies. Next, the troops had to improve the trenches and defensive positions since their defensive positions were made of mud, board, and sandbags. Third, those not on watch or making improvements needed to rest and be ready for their shift observing the enemy. Everybody needed to keep his head down below the trenches.

The first day passed without incident. At midnight, a second group, Company L, took its place to the left of Company I. Section by section, the Americans were replacing the French on the front

---

15. Keegan, *The First World War*, 175–177.

lines. After the 2nd Company took the front, the Germans began to do reconnaissance. The Americans heard the planes before they saw them, biplanes circling above with their single engines propelling them at speeds up to 100 mph, undoubtedly taking pictures and reporting troop positions back to headquarters. The French let loose several noisy salvos with their anti-aircraft guns, but to no effect. The German planes continued on unabated. Following the airplanes came intermittent shelling from the German lines, and while this caused Americans to cinch up their helmets and press tightly against the side of the trenches, there were no casualties.

As it grew dark, the men in the observation post hundreds of yards into No Man's Land moved back toward their lines for increased safety. About midnight, Private Joseph W. Guyton was ordered to fire his gun intermittently at the German trenches. The first few thrilling salvos were unanswered, but when the Germans finally responded with a machine gun barrage, Guyton was showing just enough of his head to be vulnerable. One German bullet hit him in the temple, knocking him off his feet and killing him instantly. Roy, a few hundred yards behind Guyton's post, heard the gunfire and cries for help. The first casualty of the 126th and 32nd Regiments in France had just happened. Word spread quickly, and the shocked American soldiers all kept their heads a little lower.

The next day, his comrades mournfully buried Guyton with full military honors in the little churchyard in the village of Gildwiller, less than a mile from where he fell. The French, eager to show gratitude to their young American allies, conferred Guyton with the Croix de Guerre. The official announcement and the medal were forwarded to Guyton's wife, noting that he was the first to "fall fighting for the cause of right and liberty . . . beside his French comrades." Soon after Guyton fell, Roy's commanding officer informed Company K that they would be moving to the front. In the dark, they moved through the zigzag trenches from support to the front lines, replacing the now one-man-short Company I.

With some amount of apprehension, Roy took his place in the front lines. He put his pack down in one of the recessed hollows of the trench and stepped up to the fire step, peering across No Man's Land in the dark. Strapped on his hip was his revolver, and in his hand was his Springfield rifle. He was a long way from Grand Rapids, and one of his comrades had already paid the ultimate price.

As the day slowly dawned, the Germans, suspecting that the Americans had moved into the line, began stepping up sniper fire and sent planes low over the trenches observing what they could. They also sent over a raiding party. Leading a detachment of Company K to the forward observation post in No Man's Land, Charles Cunningham was cut off from the rest of his men by Germans on an intelligence gathering raid. Instead of surrendering as he probably should have, Cunningham pulled out his pistol and began firing. The raiding party returned fire, knocking him down. Before Cunningham fell unconscious, he fired six more shots at the raiding party, driving them off. The rest of his detachment quickly converged on his position and carried him back behind the lines. Cunningham held on for over a month at a Belfort hospital, but eventually succumbed to his wounds on July 3.[16]

Four hours after the German raid, an enemy observation balloon appeared in the skies above. At 5:30 a.m., two more appeared. Two German planes flew over their lines next, and half an hour later, a French plane was observed doing reconnaissance of its own.

---

16. Gansser, *History of the 126th*, 70, and Roy Blanchard Diary, 3 July.

At 8:00 a.m., the artillery began. Back and forth for the next four hours, the Germans fired across No Man's Land at American positions, and the French Artillery in support of the American lines returned the favor. Intermittently, planes would fly low over the trenches to inspect the damage done. The soldier manning the log book noted shells on the right, shells on the left, and then shells immediately over their position. The Germans had found the range. Worse yet, some of the incoming shells were gas shells.[17]

Roy was beginning to experience what he had only heard about from the French and British officers who had led his training. War on the Western Front was an artillery war. The French had initiated the modern artillery competition years before with the *French 75*. When it had been introduced in 1898, it had rendered all other artillery obsolete. It could easily fire fifteen aimed rounds a minute, and under some conditions, fire twice that rate. Accurate and equipped with time fuses and enclosing 200–300 anti-personnel lead or steel ball shrapnel, it was designed to bounce once, explode about six feet off the ground, and blow opposing infantry to shreds.[18] From the time the *French 75* was introduced, whole companies of men could be killed, blown up, and buried without ever seeing the enemy.

This morning, for the first time on the front lines, Roy heard the faraway German guns open up, the *whizz-bang* of the quick-firing guns and the *krump* of the heavy howitzer. As the guns opened up in the distance, Roy and the soldiers of the 126th scrambled for cover, knowing that the high-caliber shells could unleash massive shrapnel or blow any exposed man or machine to bits.

---

17. *History of the 126th*, 71–72.

18. Peter Doyle, *World War I in 100 Objects* (New York: Plume, 2014), 125, 151.

The faraway moan grew to a scream, followed by a ground shaking smash and a diabolical red light . . . everybody simply shakes and crawls . . . falling trees, screams, the flop-flop of gas shells; white faced men digging like mad or standing up under it according to their temperament—some cool, some shaking, some weeping; a few grim jokes, but mostly just dull endurance; a hunching of the shoulders when another comes, and the thought—"How long, how long?" There is nothing to do. Whether you get through or not is just sheer chance and nothing more. You may and you may not.[19]

Hours of bombing with the possibility of being blown to bits, buried alive, or being blown off their feet paralyzed many with fear. It is estimated that seventy percent of all casualties on the Western Front were from shellfire. As the shells fell, Roy tried to think of home, shake the hysteria with flippant humor, or just light a cigarette with shaking hands.[20] Being shelled was like a nightmare. One soldier described it as "distant thunder, countless shells falling like rain, towers of smoke, fire, explosions, confusion, cries of help, all of it madness."[21]

The artillery on the Western Front didn't have to hit you to

19. Allen Hervey, *Toward the Flame* (New York: Farar & Rhinehart, 1926), 43–45, 48. Quoted in Hallas, *Doughboy War*, 174.

20. Roy Blanchard, Undated diary entry. "Acknowledgments of thanks to Mr. Frank Dealy of 2913 Col. Ave, Phila., Pa. For a kind donation of tobacco received while greatly in need and amid bursting shells."

21. A soldier at the battle of Verdun said, "During heavy bombardments and attacks I have seen shells falling like rain. Countless towers of smoke remind one of Gustave Dore's picture of the fiery tombs of the arch-heretics in 'Dante's Hell.'" Alistair Horne, *The Price of Glory: Verdun 1916* (New York: Macfadden, 1964), 176.

debilitate you. It simply had to explode near you often enough to destroy your nerves. The emotional toll, now called post-traumatic stress disorder (PTSD), was descriptively referred to as shell-shock and took only a few hours of shelling to develop.

"Shell-shock" was used as a generic description that covered any sort of psychiatric casualty.[22] It was a form of hysteria, an emotional state that converted into a physical one. Some of the less severe symptoms included nightmares, insomnia, or panic attacks. Extreme cases would include paralysis or the inability to talk. The intensity of this experience and regular occurrence for the next five months on the front lines revisited Roy off and on for the rest of his life. The shelling broke many men's sanity, permanently. Roy held it together while in France, but years later in Grand Rapids, he revisited these horrific days, nightmares of shells exploding, screams of long-dead comrades ringing in his ears, waking up trembling—telling himself he was safe, and it was just a dream.

For the present, Roy and the 126th made themselves small during the shelling. After the shelling lifted, Roy's regiment sent out a large working party to replace seventy-five yards of barbed wire cut to pieces during the barrage. They also alertly sent out patrols in case the shelling was the first step in a German raid.[23]

As Roy, the 126th and the 32nd were experiencing their first days of trench warfare, the 1st Division carried out the first American advance of the war. On the morning of May 27, 1918, the 1st prepared to launch their planned offensive supported by French artillery. Refusing to be distracted by Ludendorff's latest offensive, the Americans charged ahead without sufficient

---

22. Martin Gilbert, *The First World War*, 275.

23. Gansser, *History of the 126th*, 73.

French artillery support. For the first day, they achieved all of their objectives, reporting only light casualties. The Germans, surprised by the attack and not convinced the town had significant strategic value, largely withdrew or surrendered to the rash Americans. Foreshadowing the brutal warfare in months to come, the Americans found that capturing an objective was often easier than holding it. What the Americans would soon painfully discover was that the German artillery had their front lines sighted in, and when the American advance halted and began to dig in, the Germans simply blew those known positions to fine particles of mud.

The Germans believed that they could teach the Americans a lesson and continued the bombardment for seventy-two hours. Surprisingly, the determined Americans held the line. Their commanding officer, Bullard, wrote later, "It was a demonstration to the world of what was to be expected of the Americans."[24] This stubborn refusal to play by the established rules of artillery warfare cost the Americans two hundred officers and men killed and missing, and 669 wounded in the span of three days. Tragically, this was just the beginning of suffering for the American soldiers in France.

While the 1st Division was taking and holding territory at great cost, Roy's division continued to learn the basics of trench warfare. Since information on upcoming enemy advances or reinforcements could alter the course of battles, each side conducted regular raids. On June 1, the French instructed the Americans how to conduct a proper raid on a German trench. It all started at 9:00 p.m. as Roy and the 126th watched five French planes fly toward the enemy lines. After a signal from the French lines, they separated. Immediately,

---

24. Robert Lee Bullard, *Personalities and Reminiscences of the War*, 174.

the American and French artillery opened up on a 600 square yard segment of the German trenches. The Americans hadn't seen or heard anything like the intense shelling unleashed on that sector. After five minutes, the raiding party went over the top of the trench following a curtain of shells that slowly moved its way across the six-hundred yards to the German positions. The Germans frantically sent up rockets of different colors, calling for assistance and alerting their comrades to the raid. The raiding party made its way slowly through the wire entanglements that crisscrossed the pockmarked mud. The artillery fire kept the Germans' heads down and the raiding party split up as they reached the German trenches according to their prearranged plan. Minutes later, the raiding party emerged with three German prisoners. Unfortunately for the raiding party, German artillery finally responded when the raiding party was almost safely back to the American lines. Two French privates were killed before they could make it back to safety.[25]

As serious as it was to those killed in the process, the opposing armies made capturing prisoners nearly a sport on the front lines. Germans normally mastered the game and would occasionally even capture couriers carrying mail to or from a unit. The typical assault transpired as follows: first came an early morning artillery barrage, hundreds of heavy artillery firing in a cascade of deafening roars and descending tons of metal. The barrage took the shape of a box, surrounding a platoon of soldiers effectively cutting them off from any support from the rear or sides. Machine guns would fire simultaneously over the heads of those taking cover in the trenches from the shells. The assault troops would leap from their positions and start across toward the enemy position. Bangalore

25. Gansser, *History of the 126th*, 73–74.

torpedoes blasted a path through the wire, as the side of the box barrage nearest the approaching troops vanished.[26] Deafened and disorientated by the roar of shells around them, the platoon was not aware of the assault until grenades from enemy soldiers landed among them. Then the assault group followed the grenades with knives, pistols, and bayonets, capturing as many stunned prisoners as possible and dragging them back to their lines as the box barrage closed again and then ceased. This procedure was repeated up and down the line at any point that the forces desired intelligence information. The "game" normally began and ended in the space of three minutes.[27]

The French, satisfied with the American's military ability in the trenches, gave the nearly seven kilometers of the front lines to defend. What the Germans had feared, a functional American army on the Western Front, was taking shape.

---

26. A tube of sheet iron, with a conical wooden head, filled with high explosives; used to destroy wire and other obstacles to advance. Named after the Engineer Depot in Bangalore, India where the British developed the weapon. Thomas E. Griess, ed, *The Great War, The West Point Military History Series* (Wayne: Avery, 1986), 213.

27. Stallings, *The Doughboys*, 38–39.

CHAPTER 6

★ ★ ★ ★ ★

TIGHTROPE

Listen, sis, don't believe all those things you read about us in the paper. Some crepe hanger wants to hang gloom on the world and get his handle and face in the paper.

Don't ever put my letters in the paper because someone will get the idea, that this is a circus. Well I'll admit we are walking a pretty tightrope.
—ROY, LETTER TO PEARL, 11 JULY 1918

─────── ★ ★ ★ ★ ★ ───────

ONE OF THE surprising realities about the Western Front was that intense action and peril were surrounded by long periods of having very little to do. For Roy and the members of the 126th, long periods of silence broke up the irregular raids, dark nights, and artillery duels. Because of those long periods of boredom, the front-line trenches in quiet areas became coveted assignments. The men dug little holes in the sides of the trenches and often rolled up and took long naps during the daytime. In order to make it to the relative ease of daylight hours, however, the soldiers had to make it through their serious responsibilities at night.

Because of the real and present danger of machine-gun fire, snipers, and artillery men on the front line kept under cover unless there was reason to man the parapet. The exception to this general rule was the lookouts. During daylight hours, the lookouts used periscopes and counted on their ears as much as their eyes. German machine gunners had already proved to the Americans that sticking your head up above the parapet might well be the last thing a soldier ever did. In order to have an adequate warning of German forward activities, the Americans counted on the lookout and listening posts that extended nearly halfway into No Man's Land. The lookouts listened for enemy advances, raids, and the sounds of German's tunneling toward their lines.

Fortunately for the guards, it was no easy task advancing through No Man's Land, especially without making a sound. Barbed wire was typically passed through dark paint to keep it from reflecting light and then loosely strung between spaced wooden posts to provide an effective high obstacle. Strung low and tight were alarm traps—wire attached to some noisemaker that alerted the guards to movement. Sometimes, the Americans made wire entanglements by wrapping barbed wire around a long, rectangular wood frame behind the lines. These could be quickly rolled out into No Man's Land after an artillery barrage had cut a wide hole in the wire. The wire obstacles added to the chaotic and dangerous morass. Due to constant shelling, there was an irregular pattern of shell holes, thick mud, and the rotting remains of men and animals.

Despite the obstacles in No Man's Land, serving as a lookout was hell on the young men's nerves. They watched for hours in the still of the night. On occasion, they jumped at the *rat-a-tat-tat* of the machine gun, distant boom of a cannon, or sharp explosion of a hand grenade. Even the lonely rifle shots seemed much louder than normal in the awful quiet. They listened for wire cutters, shovels working underground, or the rattle of a tin can tied to a tight wire.

Roy's first night on guard duty started with a tap on the shoulder from the man he would replace. He awoke and grabbed his rifle and looked it over in the moonlight. Any item that might make noise he left with his pack. Quietly, he made his way to the covered listening post—three-feet deep and five-feet tall with a small opening in the front. It was surrounded by sandbags and loose dirt.

The night was eerily quiet. Back and forth, he scanned the darkness. Was that a movement? Was that a mound of dirt or a German soldier? It was impossible to tell at twenty yards away in the dark. To his right, was that a soldier? Only one way to tell. It was better to be safe than sorry. Roy squeezed off a shot with his .30 caliber Springfield rifle. The shot was deafening in the small, covered listening post. Fellow sentinels called out, "What did you see?" Roy answered, "I thought I saw something. But it didn't move after I shot it." Recalling his time on the Texas border and shooting coyotes, Roy chided himself.

But it wasn't just the green American soldiers firing at nothing in the dark. The Germans were jittery as well, and nervous sentries would fire off a flare to illuminate No Man's Land or fire into the weeds, bushes, or wire entanglement posts. After two hours of intense watching, Roy would report to his sergeant what he had seen on his watch, wake his replacement, and then do his best to rest.

Daytime had its own perils. The threat of German snipers kept everyone's head down, but also prevented any work getting done above the level of the trenches. The men kept their heads below the parapet of the trench and spent their days sleeping, eating, and talking with chums, sketching on diary pages, or writing letters home.[1] In these quiet sector moments, Roy wrote to Pearl. From the moment he had arrived in France, he decided that in his letters home he would trivialize the danger he faced and reassure his loved ones that he wasn't giving up his Midwest convictions. To keep things light, he made up stories, joked about cowards who couldn't summon the courage to go "over the top," and assured his sister he wasn't interested in French women.

French women distracted and amused the either stressed or bored American teens. The Army, not amused, saw them as a dangerous distraction and took significant steps to keep the soldiers from the threat of venereal disease (VD). General Pershing himself determined that VD was one of the most serious problems confronting the Medical Corps, and he took steps to prevent careless promiscuity. Enlisted men heard lectures from officers who threatened those infected with VD with court-martial or loss of pay. The official warnings against careless fraternizing with

---

1. Hallas, *Doughboy War*, 64.

women began with the first day the officers met with draftees and continued on throughout the training camps and even in the war zone.[2] The Non-Governmental Organizations (NGOs), like the YMCA and the Knights of Columbus, also admonished soldiers to remain faithful to their girls back home. Roy reminded Pearl regularly that he only had eyes for Mildred.

Despite the Army's efforts, the first troops that arrived in cosmopolitan Paris made headlines for all the wrong reasons. At France's insistence, soldiers sailed for France six months early—before the Army had organized its anti-vice programs. It wasn't long before American troops discovered the houses of prostitution, and the salacious headlines made it into the pages of the newspapers back home. By the time Roy arrived in France, the Army had successfully restrained its men, or perhaps restrained reporters. Either way, damaging stories stayed out of the papers for the most part. Instead, the papers commented on the serious training the soldiers were undertaking. The papers applauded the soldiers' efforts to learn trench warfare and proudly reported that the French trainers were impressed with the American's skill at throwing bombs (grenades). It seems as if the national pastime made the soldiers particularly accurate.[3]

Roy also successfully avoided the distraction of alcohol, most of the time. The United States, in a prohibition mood, encouraged its soldiers to choose good health and sobriety over indulging in alcohol. Regulations forbade soldiers from buying or accepting as gifts whiskey, brandy, champagne, liquors, or any other alcoholic

2. Penn Borden, *Civilian Indoctrination of the Military: World War I and Future Implications for the Military-Industrial Complex* (New York: Greenwood, 1989), 106-116.

3. *Evening Star*, Washington, D.C., 28 July 1917.

beverages besides light wines or beer. France, which served wine like the Americans served water, was annoyed by these regulations but, nonetheless, the Americans stood by their policies. After the war, Major General Robert Lee Bullard of the 1st Division, bragged,

As to morality, this subject had indeed been preached and enforced from the first with so much persistence throughout the American Expeditionary Forces that never in history has there come out of war as clean a body of men as the Americans who served in those forces in Europe.[4]

With wine and women off-limits, the troops were given more wholesome options like band concerts, moving pictures, and digging trenches. The French, who took cover when the weather worsened, found it amusing that the Americans dug in rain or shine. But, the Americans needed to dig. The trenches were in need of constant repair and improvement as the occasional bombardment from the Germans illustrated.

Roy and the 126th had very little warning when shells were coming. Needing cover, the Americans had continued to maintain and improve the system of dugouts created by the French a short distance to the rear of the front lines. These dugouts connected to the front line and communication trenches through deep tunnels. The dugouts themselves were from twelve to eighteen-feet deep below the surface and protected the soldiers from all but the heaviest German shells. The heavy German shells could penetrate as deep as twenty-five feet and did occasionally hit a dugout.

Just that type of nightmare scenario hit the 126th on June 19. At dawn, the shells began to fall and the 126th quickly retreated

---

4. Robert Lee Bullard, *Personalities and Reminiscences of the War* (New York: Doubleday, 1925), 319.

underground. Shell after shell hit the lines that Roy had occupied just days earlier. One of the heavy German shells penetrated the dugouts of unlucky Company D. The massive explosion killed two privates and wounded eight more. Fortunately, Roy's company had been moved back from that very sector to a support position. Instead of being blown to pieces, Roy was in the support sector lying under an apple tree. He took the moment to write to Pearl.

Some Where In France

Dearest Sister

I will try to write you a line now that I have a little time to myself.

Am feeling fine and hope everyone at home is the same.

It sure is summer here. The sun is hot and the fields are very pretty. At present I am lying under an apple tree in a small orchard, flat on my stomach. It sure seems good to get out of the trenches and rest up a little.

I hear from Mildred quite often and she is well. You can just bet I'd like to be home to-day and I have had my fill of war, but as we are here to see the thing thru, I've got to stick to it and do my best. I wouldn't give a franc for this whole country if I had to live here.

I am billeted in an old stone barn now and the rats (a foot long) are awful friendly. I have not been bothered by cooties much, but it takes a lot of scrubbing to keep away from them.

Bert Zuff is back from the hospital and only has a scar about six inches long. He is proud of it.

Do you remember Corp. Drake? The short fellow that went to Creston park with us to see that baseball game last summer? He is writing to a girl friend of his at Kidd Key College, Tex.

I haven't got time for the girls here. They are very scarce up here and are not so pretty as they say and are not worth noticing. Last night I heard our old band play and saw some YMCA movies. Gee it seemed good to be in some what civilized life again. I wish I could see your new home now. I'll bet you just shook up things right. Listen if mother wants any money for anything, tell her she can use mine if she cares to.

Try to hang on to the piano if you can, until I get back.

It is very hard to get any tobacco around here only the little that they issue. If I knew how to send for some I would ask for it, but some say we must fill out blanks.

We have not been paid yet this month so if steam boats sold for 5 cents a dozen, I couldn't buy the echo of the whistle. Will try to send you a souvenir when we get paid.

I suppose you know that the French do not measure distance by feet, yards or miles. No it is the metric system. "Too many kilometers to there." A kilometer is about 5/8 of a mile.

I never get bawled up in centimes or francs anymore and really I never see any US money.

My French tongue is developing quite rapidly, but I do not care so much about it as I did at first.

I sure am taking on weight and height. Now, I weigh about 156 lbs and am 67 3/8" tall.

Well Sis, dear, I must close now, but hope soon to hear from you.

Write soon.
Your loving Brother
Corp. Roy Blanchard
Co.K 126th Inf.
<u>*American*</u> *E. F.*
(notice)

Although Roy could get away from the trenches once in awhile, he could not easily escape the rats and cooties. Rats, the only creatures that seemed to flourish in the trenches, were quite brave and were often a foot long (not including the tail), the size of a small cat. They grew fat on the corpses in No Man's Land and were known to bite sleeping soldiers' faces and gather around the eating areas.[5] The French left the rats alone. Like a canary in a coal mine, the rats were a warning that gas shells had been fired. At the slightest whiff of gas, the large rats flipped feet up, dead. The Americans hated them too much to leave them alone. They bludgeoned the rats with shovels and rifle butts or shot them with their side arms.

Lice, or "cooties," were also a constant companion of soldiers on the Western Front. One soldier noted that "they added to the soldier's troubles, subtracted from his pleasures, divided his attention and multiplied like hell."[6] They looked like small potato bugs, laid eggs in the seams of soldiers' underwear and uniforms, and multiplied rapidly, aided by the soldiers' body heat. They were blood-sucking insects, and their activities formed little sores and scabs all over the body and caused an almost unbearable itch. Soldiers tried to get rid of them by squeezing them between their thumbnails and went over the seams of their clothing with matches, candles, or cigarette lighters. If troops were behind the lines, they could put their clothes in a big steam delouser, but that protection only lasted a few days at best.[7] Roy complained little, and primarily joked about them, which was a common enough reaction to problems that everyone had and no one could get rid of.

As if lousy critters and bugs weren't enough, the Americans also

5. Hallas, *Doughboy War,* 65.

6. Ibid., 66.

7. Ibid., 84.

suffered from disorganized supply lines. Roy periodically went without solid meals for days on end. Sometimes, a hot meal was enough of an event to warrant a diary entry. A growling stomach and constant rain made the Yanks miss home all the more. On June 20, Roy's hungry Company K relieved the battered Company D in the lines. Many of Company K was sick, but there was nothing to do but bear it. Rats and cooties, illness, and lack of food were annoying, but the real enemy lay across No Man's Land.

Early on June 23, the real enemy struck two sectors over from Roy's post. The Germans, camouflaged with grass on their helmets and bodies, succeeded in getting close enough to reach out and touch the Americans before they were detected. One of the Germans shot Lieutenant Carl Johnson in the gut. The confused and startled Americans stared as the whole parapet of the trench seemed to be rising up against them. The three dozen Germans then commenced throwing "potato masher" grenades, cutting off three Americans from the rest of their company. The Germans demanded the three Americans surrender. The Americans, unused to the normal practice of trench warfare, rudely declined their offer. Ducked down and with their backs against the front of the trenches, they fired their rifles at any German movement and fought with grim determination. One large German peaked too far over the trench and was shot, toppling head first into the trench. Private Newton Bell viciously hammered the German's skull with his iron rifle-grenade discharger until he stopped moving. The Americans then tossed grenades in the general direction of the Germans and finally, amid the explosions, sprinted away, dashing bit by bit the 350 yards back to their main trenches.[8]

---

8. Gansser, *History of the 126th*, 78–79.

As they were nearing their lines, the Germans let loose a thirty-five-minute barrage accompanied by heavy machine-gun fire. The Americans in the main trenches took cover and fired rockets into the early morning sky, calling for a counter barrage. No counter barrage came. Next, they sent runners to the Company Post of Command in desperation, despite the danger to those messengers in the middle of murderous shell-fire, giving reports about the raid.

While the Germans focused on one sector of the line, four hundred yards to the right, Americans spotted the enemy raiding party still in No Man's Land. They opened fire, wounding two Germans and driving the raiding party back. The Americans pressed forward as quickly as possible, hoping to rescue Lieutenant Johnson. Instead, they found his lifeless body with one bullet in his stomach and one in the forehead. As they began to move Johnson's body, one of the soldiers noticed wires and unusual bulges. The Germans had rigged Johnson's corpse with all manner of explosives, including grenades and dynamite. Deciding to risk deactivating the bombs, they carefully removed the explosives and brought Johnson's body back to their lines. The Germans had also stripped Johnson's uniform of articles of identification and removed his leather leggings, presumably to receive the German bonus for killing an Allied officer.

Johnson's death infuriated the 126th. Johnson was a popular officer and the first officer in the division to die on the front. The cruelty of stripping the body for bounty and booby trapping it with explosives reminded the men of the various war crimes that had convinced them to volunteer. The men constructed a concrete vault for Johnson and laid him to rest on the side of a hill outside Soppe-le-Bas after a somber march through town. At the burial site, the men bowed their heads in respect to their fallen comrade. The chaplain reminded the young men that Johnson fought and died so that democracy and freedom might not perish from the earth. His words were sporadically interrupted by German shells whizzing and whining overhead. The shells exploded harmlessly a hundred yards away, but the soldiers swore they would remember this final indignity. Their time of avenging the loss of their brother in arms would come; of that they were certain.[9]

In the meantime, they waited.

Some weeks brought nothing but rain. Sickness was common, and the trenches became nearly intolerable. The duck-boards kept their feet mostly dry but the soldiers on the front line could not escape the mud. Thankfully, they were regularly cycled back from the front lines to support positions.

When they did get time behind the lines, they found diversion where they could. It was in one of these times that Roy discovered gambling, and he did quite well at first. On June 27, he won eighteen francs. The next night, he won twenty-eight francs. Roy kept notes in his diary on the price of various items in town, and his winnings could have bought eight bottles of champagne or nine dozen eggs.[10]

As exciting as besting his comrades in poker was, nothing compared to observing French artillery fire. Roy had experienced being on the receiving end of shellfire, but being on the firing end was exhilarating. While his company was in support positions, he could observe the heavy artillery pounding the hated Germans. The roar of the artillery and the surreal puff of smoke at the end of the trajectory made for a spectacular sight.

Not all of his time in support was without danger. Roy

---

9. Ibid., 80. Roy Blanchard diary, June 22–24.

10. Roy Blanchard diary, 9 July 1918. He stated that champagne was 5.50 francs per bottle, and eggs were five francs a dozen.

spent several days doing the very dangerous duty of delivering food to men on the front lines. The mud and shell holes made transportation of food by motor car to the front lines difficult, if not impossible. Horses, unable to take cover at the warning whistle of a shell, were rarely used. Men were therefore assigned to the duty. At active sectors, German artillery trained their guns on familiar supply paths and sent shells over at regular intervals. Roy darted in quick spurts, kept his head down, and made his way back and forth between support and the front lines delivering valuable supplies.

The fastest manned vehicle on the Western Front was the remarkable new flying machine. Aircraft, particularly tethered balloons, had been used in previous wars, but the usefulness and rapid evolution of flying machines surprised military experts at the beginning of the war. Since World War I was an artillery war and an exercise in getting troops and equipment mobilized quickly, the Generals on both sides of the conflict quickly understood the value of aerial surveillance. Biplanes quickly replaced cavalry. Even the skeptics were convinced by the work that the British pilots did in discovering German troop movements in the early weeks of the war. The intelligence delivered to high command kept the British from being surrounded and saved an estimated 100,000 British lives. Weeks later, at the pivotal First Battle of Marne, airplane reconnaissance revealed weak points and exposed flanks in the German lines. The precise counter-attacks by French and British stopped the German advance and turned the war into a stalemate.[11]

---

11. http://www.centennialofflight.net/essay/Air_Power/WWI-reconnais sance/AP2.htm, accessed February 10, 2015.

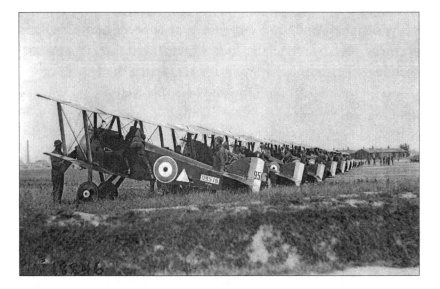

American Pilots Preparing for Takeoff

As trenches began to stretch from Switzerland to the ocean, both sides saw the value of keeping regular check on troop movements and developing trench systems. The airplanes became spotters for the artillery and the eyes and ears for the high command. Naturally, the opposing side wanted to knock them down. Opposing pilots brought pistols in the air to take shots at the other planes. If out of ammo, the pilots would throw whatever else was in the cockpit—bricks, grenades, or even rope that they hoped might entangle the enemy's propeller. The early pilots avoided heavy guns at first because the relatively flimsy airplanes could become easily unbalanced. Some also feared shooting one's own tail or wing off as they were firing at enemies. Over time, balance issues were solved and the French were the first to successfully mount a machine gun that could be aimed by pointing the nose of the aircraft at the enemy. The next innovation was to mount steel deflector wedges so the pilots wouldn't shoot off their own propeller. The Germans, led by designer Anthony Fokker, made planes even more deadly to opposing pilots by connecting the trigger to the timing of the engine, enabling the pilot to steer and fire easier. In the static fields of the Western Front, absent of horses or saber-led charges, the mobile, spiraling, single-engine airplanes spitting fire and risking doom captivated both the attention of their fellow soldiers and readers back home. Newspaper writers and politicians treated the pilots as "knights" of the war. They flew fast and dangerous maneuvers in order to defend critical artillery observation balloons. They battled other pilots either one-on-one or in squadrons, fought like heroes, and died in droves. France alone produced at least 68,000 aircraft, of which 52,000 were lost in battle.[12] The planes reached speeds of over 100 mph and fired machine guns, pistols, or rockets at each other. The winners sped away; the losers spiraled to the earth.[13]

Even in the heat of battle, men stopped to watch the dogfights in the sky above their trenches. Roy couldn't get enough of the airplanes, filling his diary with pictures and describing them to Pearl in his letters home. Most mornings, the scouting planes circled low over the 126th an hour before daylight, noting the American movements, and suggesting targets to the ever-ready artillery. Despite the danger it represented, Roy gaped at the daring pilots flying over 100 mph overhead. The triplanes like the Fokker Dr.1 were nearly nineteen feet in length with a twenty-three-foot wingspan and seemed to effortlessly defy every attack from the anti-aircraft guns that tried to knock them out of the sky.

12. http://www.firstworldwar.com/airwar/summary.htm, accessed July 31, 2015.

13. Horne, *The Price of Glory,* 199–212. Only a handful of aces survived the war.

By July 4, Roy began to hear rumors that their time in Alsace was coming to an end. They celebrated that news along with America's birthday by firing at the hated Germans. First, they cheered in unison Next, they coordinated unison firing. And finally, they heaved grenades toward the German lines.

Two days later, Roy and his company again cycled out of their front-line position to support positions near the little village of Soppe La Bas. Roy walked through and around shell hole after shell hole on his way into what was left of the village. The biggest crater stretched approximately sixteen-feet-wide and eight-feet-deep. Looking down at the size of it made him feel fortunate to have survived his first stint at the front. Several times, he had cheated death by being in the right place at the right time and he wondered how long his luck would last.

On July 7, Roy celebrated about getting sixteen letters from home. News from home lightened his mood and reminded him how much he missed his family. The normal goings on in Grand Rapids were a world apart from the danger of the trenches and the madness of life on the Western Front. Day after day, friends faced dangers from themselves and others. His friend, John Williams, was nearly killed by a jumpy sentry coming back from a patrol. Another friend reached a breaking point. First, the young man got drunk in town. He came back and stole Roy's pistol. Roy woke up to the sound of his friend hooting and hollering while emptying Roy's pistol in the air. Soldiers cautiously approached the drunk and told him to stand down. Instead of cooperating, he dropped the gun and ran after the person interfering with his fun, brandishing a trench knife. Other soldiers managed to subdue him, and Roy was able to retrieve his gun and fulfill his guard duties that evening. After guard duty, he and his bunk-mate Knittle were so tired they didn't care if their bunks were in a barn over a smelly hog pen.

July 11, 1918
In France

Dear Sister:

This is a beautiful day and it just puts the old time pep into a fellow. If you folks are all as well as I am you got something to brag about.

Well at present I am sitting in my little pup tent with my bedmate just outside. We just got to this village a couple days ago and I preferred to live in the open, instead of furnishing meat for cooties in those measly billets.

This morning I washed a suit of underwear, a shirt, three sap catchers, two pair of socks and three towels. Then I jumped in the creek and took the best bath I ever took in my career.

Well we have been in the Trenches again. It sure seems good to get out of the trenches to get a good bath, shave and a change of clothes.[14]

Did you see Lawrence Knittle's picture and letter in the paper? He is my bed mate now. How hot that sun is.

I received your letter while yet in the ditches. We couldn't write then, but yours truly is going to cut the buck with a pen for a few days now. Give all the old corner decorators my best wishes and tell them that border stuff was sure soft.

Well I suppose you are wondering how we spent the 4rth of July. We didn't spend it, it just naturally spent itself. Early in

---

14. It was a welcome relief for soldiers to get a change of clothes. Some companies went three months without a new issue of underwear. Their socks, worn day and night for months without change, would grow as hard as boards, and often crack in two while being removed. James H. Hallas, *Doughboy War*, 185.

the morning everyone must have seen Boche[15] at once or else they shut their eyes and thought they were spending 4rth of July at Reeds Lake. Well anyway we had sky rockets[16] (used to light up nobody land) and grenades. Grenades are little iron bombs that bark awfully just because you pull their pin out.

It was not as safe and sane as last year.

And the rats.

The Pied Piper never saw any rats.

They pull off entertainments every night and often a whole barrage of them make a mass attack on us. I tie everything down now.

Someone put some cheese out in tin cans hanging on the barbed wire entanglements (the cans are tied to the wire so that the slightest movement will jingle them) and at night the rats come out and it sounded like a whole regiment of Boche. Well someone heaved a grenade out there and all was left was a couple of thin squeaks.

Say, I never heard whether Fred Fulton fought or not. Will you find out and let me know, also who won the match.

Suppose you folks do not see any airplanes around there. Well if a day's skipped by without seeing one we would think the aviators all quit. Oh! It's a wonderful life—if you don't weaken.

We have discovered a new dance while under shell fire. It is called "the Dugout glide" When one hears the music begin (it begins at the mouth of some Boche cannon) then it's time to

---

15. Boche was a French term that literally meant "the hard headed ones." It also loosely translated to "beast."

16. Sky rockets were flares, used to light up "No Man's Land" and to signal artillery where to fire.

start gliding into the nearest hole available. The best dancers go home providing they don't get bumped off by a typewriter (machine gun), gassed, or slide on the end of a bayonet—or get too seasick.

There ain't enough Dutchman over there to get me, but I am going to be awfully careful of automobiles the first day I get home.

One night I thot sure I was gassed. The air in the dugouts was blue (I think) anyway I started for my mask when someone said, "Hey Curley, for God sake, go out side to take them shoes off" I won't say anything about my own feet, because I arrange to take my shoes off when eight or ten others do, then they don't holler at me.

The night we arrived in this village, Knittle and I found an unoccupied place on the upper floor of a barn and Knittle crawled up first. He sniffed then he listened. Then he said he was positive there were pigs up there. Well the truth was, pigs were snorting and snoring in a pen about five feet under us and the odor was dazing. But a couple of tired trench rats will hay in most anywhere, but we had to keep cigarettes a-going until we got to sleep so the odor would not drive us to putting on our masks.

Listen, sis, don't believe all those things you read about us in the paper. Some crepe hanger wants to hang gloom on the world and get his handle and face in the paper.

Don't ever put my letters in the paper because someone will get the idea that this is a circus. Well I'll admit we are walking a pretty tightrope.

Must close.

Your Dear Brother

Corp. Roy Blanchard

Walking a pretty tightrope indeed. Hoping not to break like his gun-stealing friend, Roy coped with life in the trenches by laughing at it or by turning it into a game of sorts. Getting shelled was a dance, rats were there to entertain, being gassed was like living with people with stinky feet. Although he resented the "glory hounds" who had their letters published in the papers, Roy admitted to his sister that his adventure was not quite the circus that he reported. He understood that reality lay somewhere between the two extremes. Just as he never despaired when his father deserted the family, Roy coped with the terror and boredom of the Western Front with a mix of courage and wit. He would laugh it off, courageously stay positive, and not think too much about the past. Amid the insanity of the Western Front, some days a soldier's duty was to cope by frivolity: "The only thing to do is laugh at everything. Keep jolly, make fun of it all. . . . Give absurd names to everything."[17]

A week after reporting all of this madness to Pearl, Roy's 126th was on the move again. The Alsace had been labeled a quiet area but had cost many of Roy's friends their lives. Chateau-Thierry was an active front. The courage that had fortified Roy in Alsace would be tested in the days ahead.

---

17. Persico, *11th Month, 11th Day, 11th Hour,* 106.

★ ★ ★ ★ ★

AN ACTIVE SECTOR

Boche, French and Yanks dead in woods . . .
—Roy Blanchard diary, 29 July 1918

★ ★ ★ ★ ★

THE MUDDY, RAT-INFESTED trenches were miserable, but they were life amid the machine guns, sniper fire, and shelling. That's why Roy had mixed feelings when he and the 126th were ordered to train their replacements, pack their gear, and slip silently out of their quiet sector. Their peaceful sector hadn't been so quiet of late. Some nights, the Germans let loose artillery barrages at 3:00 a.m., and everyone in the trenches, except for the lookouts, stumbled in the dark to the dugouts. Occasionally, the barrages would last over an hour—shell after screaming shell to the right, left, or right on top of them.

Faking bravado only got one so far. After an hour of shelling, it just became mental endurance. It helped Roy a little bit to reach into his pocket for a cigarette in the suffocating dugout. Sometimes he would think of what he would be doing if he had turned down the National Guard offer all those months ago.

The casualties kept building in the regiment: some from shelling and some from machine gun fire. Many were killed on raids; others died while hunched together as huge German shells blew a dugout to pieces. The morning they left Alsace, the total casualties in the 126th regiment had mounted to over 400 men, including several from Company K. Roy solemnly wrote down his fallen friends' names on the page of his small diary alongside the date of their passing. As they left the trenches in Alsace, he looked toward where they buried 1st Lt. Johnson. The next sector would be much more dangerous, his commanding officer promised.

On the other side of the lines, the German high command read reports and fretted. The spring offensives had run their course and failed to meet their ambitious but necessary objectives. Germany had flung the last of its best men at the British lines from March to July, and while they made progress early, the British had managed to hold on, strengthened by the inexperienced Americans. The Germans who had personally encountered the Americans found them determined, brave to the point of reckless, and too numerous to count. The French and British admitted to themselves that the Americans were strangely inspiring. The crazy Yanks sang on the way to battle, dug trenches in the rain, and refused to retreat.

Perhaps the most encouraging part of the American arrival was their sheer numbers. The British, French, and Germans were all long past the point where they could replace military age men. The Germans had already conscripted every capable man in their empire. Now, their divisions—undermanned and partially filled with young, old, and injured—were all they had left. While the Americans landed 250,000 troops each month in France, the German Army had shrunk from 5.1 million to 4.2 million men in the last six months, and many of those who were left were undependable, wounded, or poorly trained.[1]

As the Americans brought new inspiration to the Allies, the Germans were losing theirs. The spring offensives cost the Germans hundreds of thousands of casualties, including national hero pilot Manfred von Richthofen, the Red Baron. Hope for a decisive German victory was slipping away. Persistently, the Germans had fortified their lines for nearly four years. They put their hope in a stalemate that would force the Americans to make peace without victory. To accomplish this, the Germans planned to make the Allies pay dearly for every yard of French mud they recaptured.

The 32nd Division, including Roy's 126th Regiment, was sent

1. John Keegan, *The First World War* (Knopf: New York, 1999), 397–409.

to take back that land from the German invaders. Together with the 1st, 2nd, 3rd, 4th, 26th, 28th, 42nd Divisions and the French, the 32nd was taking part in a massive counter-attack against the Germans. If they were successful, they would drive the Germans back to their positions behind the Vesle and Aisne Rivers.

As part of the massive 32nd Division's move north, the 126th marched toward the train station row after row in common cadence. The lines that stretched for miles were full of men in khaki uniforms, perfect except for the clinging dust, their helmets strapped tightly under their chins, eyes forward, and step spirited. Lined up at the station were French trains with forty-nine to fifty cars each. For the next forty-eight hours, the 32nd Division would embark in segments. Every four hours, a train left the station packed with men and supplies. As Roy marched up to the train depot, he noticed the new flatcars that had been added to their long line of boxcars. Mounted on the flatcars were anti-aircraft guns. The guns were familiar—the same guns that had been ineffective against the German triplanes on the front lines—but at least they could fire back. Company K split up and crowded aboard the boxcars. Although they claimed to fit forty men or eight horses, Roy's boxcar managed only thirty-six men, one box of hard tack, and thirteen cans of beans. Roy could either sit uncomfortably on the ground or stand up and look out one of the windows at the top. The train whistled, and they clanked forward. On and on, the train rumbled down the tracks past Belfore, Langres, Chaumont, Troyes, Sens, Motereau, and Paris.

At the sight of Paris, the young men got up and crowded the windows of the cramped train car. Roy gazed at the ancient walls of Paris and caught a glimpse of the Eiffel Tower. Excited Parisians at the train station waved handkerchiefs and flags, and cheered the Americans zipping by. The trains kept on for the thirty-two-hour ride. They derailed forty kilometers northeast from Paris and in the rear of the Compiegne Front. Roy stiffly stepped off the boxcar in the little town of Verberie. He could see French observation balloons in the distance—the front was only fifteen kilometers ahead.

The American soldiers' billet, or temporary lodging, was miles away from the station. After a few minutes of stretching, they set off toward Villers-Saint-Frambourg. The 126th marched on well-worn ground. France had sent soldiers down this same road in 1914, stopping the German advance and forcing the war into a stalemate. They marched all day without food and arrived at their billet at 2:00 a.m. Roy's blanket was wet, and he couldn't quiet his thoughts, tossing and turning until 5:30 a.m. or so. Before heading to bed, he caught the rumor that they would rest for a week before heading forward. That information turned out to be wrong. As the men were roused from the beds, the officers told the 126th to eat quickly, for they were moving out that morning. Roy and his comrades grimly downed the corned willie and coffee. Breakfast wasn't enough to make up for missing food the day before and certainly not enough to last the day. The 32nd was driven forward quickly, hustled toward the front lines even faster than their own supplies could travel. Again, that night Roy slept fitfully, his wet clothes, damp blanket, and soggy boots having given him a rash.

The next morning started at 6:00 a.m. and, on an empty stomach, Roy and his fellow soldiers marched 1.5 kilometers to waiting troop trucks. The whole world seemed to be moving in different directions. Roy counted endless numbers of transport trucks, tractors pulling giant artillery, lines of blue French infantry, and regiments of French troops from all corners of the globe. There were tanks mixed in line with the trucks full of bread and supplies. Giant ammunition dumps littered the side of the road. Some of the villages they rode through had been completely leveled. All that remained were signs painted on scrap wood and planted in the mud, letting the observer know what town used to occupy this space.

Past devastated towns and groves of splintered trees and crater holes, they bumped along for twelve hours. The trucks finally came to a stop at what was left of Chateau Thierry. Roy gazed over the landscape of the formerly picturesque French town. The bridge across the River Marne had been blown into small pieces by the retreating Germans. Artillery had punched holes in buildings or reduced them to piles of brick. The Germans had ransacked the town, stealing or destroying anything of value. Roy walked over and around ruined walls, stepping over bedding, clothing, children's toys, carpets, and shattered dishes. There was no time to stop and reflect, however. The 126th moved through the city as quickly as possible, crossing the River Marne on a hastily constructed French pontoon bridge. The Germans were miles away, but their artillery had a long arm. Nowhere felt safe to Roy amid the rubble and tottering buildings. Leaving the city behind, they entered the wasted countryside. Large shell holes, jagged stumps of full-grown trees, and gas residue clinging to puddles all pointed to the power of modern warfare. No living thing remained. The odor of rotting human corpses filled what was left of the woods: the dead wearing the uniforms of France, Germany, and the US.

As the burial details finished digging holes and marking graves, word passed from man to man that the Germans had left the town six days ago. The Americans needed to keep up pursuit, but they were outstretching their supply lines. That night, they had neither supper nor shelter. But they were on the trail of the Germans, and the men were too tired to complain. As they walked almost due north toward the front, the dark overcast sky made the flashes from the artillery in the distance appear all the more vivid. Roy could see, hear, and feel the artillery close by from the American batteries as they sent shell after shell into the German positions. In the distance, like lightning, the Germans fired back, a distant *krump, krump*—the shells screaming over the barren landscape, the explosion of mud, machinery, and men.

In between taking cover from the shelling, the 126th marched without talking, slowly approaching the front, lost in their own thoughts, not mindful of how close some Allied batteries were. As they passed some of the camouflaged guns in the darkness, a few of them let loose a thunderous salvo, nearly throwing the nearby 126th off their feet. Roy's company listened to the salvo and then heard someone yell, "Gas!" The 126th fumbled for their gas masks, breathing hard and straining their eyes for mist or movement. A few minutes of stress lessened as officers determined that a nervous soldier had mistaken the burning powder of their own cannons for the deadly smell of poison gas.[2]

As the 126th marched onward toward the front, they encountered wounded Americans coming the other way. Making room for them to pass, Roy watched the long lines of soldiers being transported back on stretchers toward the field hospital, some with a single, long white bandage wrapped around their head, some with limbs missing, some groaning, and others unconscious. Soberly, the 126th marched past the headless body of a Yank lying in the gutter.

The column swung into single file, with space between companies and platoons. Marching until 3:00 a.m., they stopped in a small forest, put their heavy packs on the ground, and unrolled their packs. The woods were thick. In the blackness, Roy could only see a few feet in front of him in the dark, and there wasn't

2. Gansser, *History of the 126th*, 93.

any acceptable cover. He had just put his pack down, when it started. A distant set of *krumps* went off somewhere in the distance and, moments later, the screaming shells descended, men yelled, and wood shrapnel flew from exploding trees. Roy hit the deck, grabbed his helmet, and held the fear back behind his clenched teeth. In the flash of the exploding shells, he saw his comrades and friends lying still, small, some crouched behind trees, some cursing, all helpless. Bigger shells came, shaking the landscape like a freight train speeding past a rickety station. Everything shook with diabolical red flashes and deafening roars. It went on and on, hour after hour.

Amid the madness, Roy had his duties. Not all the shells were explosive. Early during the shelling, he heard the distinct three shots in the air from a nearby Corporal of the Guard. Gas! Roy scrambled to put his mask on in the dark. Once secure, he unholstered his side arm and fired three shots into the night sky, passing the signal on to the next Corporal of the Guard. Having done his duty, he again got small and tried to stay under cover. He thought of home to calm his nerves. What was Mildred doing? How was Pearl? How did he get in the middle of this madness? Minutes passed, and the *all clear* sounded out. He took off his mask and relayed the *all clear* to the next Corporal of the Guard. Nine different times during the night, the signals went back and forth amid the 126th, three shots in the air from the Corporal of the Guard, the men scrambling for their masks and clutching their helmets as the shells fell in the thick woods.[3] In the middle of it all, Roy grinned grimly. So this was an active front.

Daylight on July 29 showed the regiment commanders just how vulnerable and close to the Germans they had marched. They felt

---

3. Ibid., 95. Roy Blanchard diary, 28-30 July 1918.

fortunate they had only nine casualties the night before. By the sound of the shells, they could tell they were under fire by the heavy field guns, the German 150s. The 113-pound shell had a range of nearly fourteen miles and flew at 2,500 feet per second. Each trained German crew could fire two or three rounds per minute. Roy's commanding officers faced reality: they couldn't stand up under that type of shelling for long without shelter. Prudently, the regiment retreated two kilometers (1.2 miles)—back to a more sheltered sector of the woods. Americans and Germans had fought here recently and had moved on quickly before burying the dead. Ghastly sights greeted the men, including one American doughboy who had died while firing his rifle from a kneeling position. His head was split in two, one part fallen on his raised arm, while his body remained kneeled.

Roy felt weak. He hadn't eaten in three days. He had hiked all night with a heavy pack. The shelling had blown his nerves, and he felt jumpy and nearly delirious.

During the day on July 29, the American and French artillery poured constant artillery fire on the Germans, and the Germans answered like a distant echo. Roy's company foraged in the woods and nearby fields, finding some potatoes to eat in addition to their reserve rations. Airplanes dueled overhead throughout the day, relaying troop positions to waiting artillery commanders. Word circulated that the Americans and French had advanced eight kilometers in the last three days, but that good news was softened by the fact that they needed to move again and that the kitchens still hadn't caught up. Their field rations were nearly gone, and Roy gulped down his bully beef, bread, beans and a little bit of sugar. He told his diary he was cheerful, like the marching song recommended: "Pack up your troubles in your old kit bag, and smile, smile, smile."

As they marched toward the front lines, smiles were hard to come by. The men counted the dead German, French, and Yanks in the woods—dozens of them, as they walked through the dense cover. Three times during the night, they donned their gas masks. They pressed on, capturing German equipment in the woods and securing a small town.

While they continued to march toward the sounds of the guns, Roy noticed fear behind the eyes of some of his fellow soldiers. Death and destruction surrounded them. Corpses in the ditches, wounded on stretchers, shell holes were everywhere. They hadn't even reached the front lines yet. The Germans were retreating for the moment in an orderly fashion, but surely they would stop and dig in where the advantage was theirs.

The 126th kept moving, hoping to press the Germans as far back as possible. Past the town of Fresnes, over the Ourcq River north of Courmont, through the northern half of Grimpettes Woods. They marched up the hill northwest of the woods and then pivoted north toward the village of Cierges. Roy's Company K was leading the 126th, as alert as they could be after the long, forced march.

The Germans waited until Roy's company entered the outskirts of the village before unloosing a long salvo of artillery shells right on top of them. Hearing the incoming shells, Roy and his company sprinted toward the only shelter in sight—the village. Huddling behind buildings, they rested for a moment. Shots rang out: one man down, another man down. Clutching their rifles, the men fanned out and looked up in the direction of the shots. One of the men saw movement in the steeple of the church. A sniper team was hiding behind a large Red Cross flag that someone had hung in the steeple. Men from Company K knelt, took aim, and peppered the steeple with bullets. The sniper fire halted, but

Company K sent up a team to confirm that the snipers were no longer a threat.

Fearing that stopping and resting would allow the Germans time to stop, dig in, and strengthen their defenses, the Americans pressed on. The Germans had left men on a prominent hill overlooking the Ourcq River, and command selected Roy's platoon to lead the assault. The commanding officer laid out the plan as dozens from the 125th and 126th quickly crossed the Ourcq River again and advanced over open ground toward the hill, labeled Hill 212. The Germans were ready for the advancing Americans. First came the shells blowing dirt and small bits of rock in the air. Roy and his comrades hit the deck. Next, the Germans opened up with their machine guns crisscrossing the open ground. There was no way forward. Roy found a shell hole for cover and huddled there with a few men until command ordered them back to their previous positions. Even after retreating, they remained pinned down by German artillery and machine-gun fire. Looking for shelter, the 125th Regiment found a mill to the rear of the front position and set it up as a first-aid station. More of a large target than shelter, the German gunners found the range and flattened the mill, killing two medical officers and fourteen wounded men. The rest of the night was spent feeling like the very earth was being ripped apart by the shock and crash of screaming shells. The men made themselves small and prayed for the dawn. The regiment had advanced two kilometers that day at the cost of five killed and fifty three wounded, including eight wounded in Roy's Company K.[4]

At 1:00 a.m. on August 1, headquarters managed to get orders to the 126th amid falling shells. Again, the orders were to advance.

---

4. Ibid., 103–4. Roy Blanchard diary, 31 July 1918.

The 126th was to renew the attack and drive the Germans out of the nearby woods. First Battalion would advance due north and attack the woods from the South. Roy's 3rd Battalion was to move toward the town of Sergy and advance across the southern slope of Hill 212 to attack the woods from the west. The maps given were worthless in the dark, and no one dared light a candle for fear of the German's concentrating fire. The officers covered one of the shell holes with jackets and tried to look at the map with lit matches, but all they managed to do was burn their fingers.

The next morning, a short salvo of artillery fire loosened up the German position in the woods at 4:00 a.m. A large segment of the 126th moved forward in skirmish lines, one behind the other, as close as they dared to the rolling barrage of artillery that went forward in front of the men. Sighting the advancing troops, the Germans let loose a strong volley of machine-gun fire. Americans fell in bunches but kept advancing under whatever cover they could find. When the Americans got close enough to the German positions, they fixed bayonets and charged, killing some, driving other Germans back, and taking dozens of prisoners. Not wanting to slow down, the first wave of infantry moved onto the next strong point, leaving the mop up to the second wave. A sergeant, part of this second wave, noticed an undamaged enemy machine gun tipped over on its side. The sergeant took a private with him and found two dead soldiers lying behind the gun with coats thrown over their faces. The sergeant deliberated for a moment and decided to take no chances. Nodding at the private, both soldiers fired into the bodies of the Germans at the same time. Both "dead" Germans cried out in pain and waved their arms, asking for mercy. Mercy was given, and the two wounded men were added to the growing number of German prisoners of war. Other men were not so easy to grant mercy to. The Germans, often selecting their best and bravest soldiers for machine gunners, tended to continue firing at the advancing Americans until further resistance was impossible. Then they would arise, throw up their hands, and shout "Kamerad." The Americans did not always let these killers surrender.

With each hill gained, with every kilometer they advanced, there were fewer men left in the regiment. No sleep, little food or water, constant shelling, little rest, horrific sights, and the smell of the dead, decaying soldiers had rattled the remaining men. After every skirmish, Roy watched wounded friends from Grand Rapids being carried on stretchers to the rear. Companies A, B, C, H, I, L, and M were badly shot up. The soldiers had terrible wounds, like those he had seen on stretchers being carried away from the battlefield days earlier. But this time they weren't strangers to be pitied—they were men from his hometown. Triplanes buzzed overhead. The Germans seemed to have full control of the skies. The men prepared for the shells they knew would come next. Company K hurriedly forged a dugout with the guns of the hated Germans thundering in the distance. Roy took cover and endured the heavy shelling at intervals throughout the night.

At dawn, the 125th and 126th lined up in their temporary trenches. There was no sense staying put, and there were no replacements for them yet. Roy looked left and right with thousands of men in khaki, dull steel helmets, standing below the parapet of the hastily dug trench facing the German lines. Roy took a moment to kick a toehold in the wall of the trench. The whistles sounded and both regiments climbed and crawled over the top in waves and trotted forward, crossing the Sergy-Cierges road under heavy machine-gun and rifle fire. The men hustled to make the cover of the trees ahead. In the distance, they could see a German observation balloon, whose operator was passing their movements to the artillery using flag signals. As the Americans entered the woods, two enemy planes flew low over the treetops. By the time the second skirmish line of American troops reached the woods, the shells began to fall. The second wave of Americans dashed through the crashing shells, barely making it to cover. The advance lines dug in feverishly: the reserve troops systematically clearing out any remaining Germans in the woods.

No sooner had the Americans mopped up the resistance when the Germans counter-attacked. First, the Germans launched a terrific barrage of artillery fire, driving most of the Americans back. After the shelling stopped, the German troops came back in waves from two directions, the Americans resisting first with rifles, then with pistols and bayonets. The Americans, overwhelmed by the superior numbers, fell back and fought their way again to the edge of the woods where the rest of the 125th and 126th covered their retreat and held the line till the following morning. The bodies of dead fighters littered the battlefield by the hundreds. Roy had never been this tired. Some of the men wandered about, muttering, while others stared off into the distance with their mouth gaping open—clearly shell-shocked. The bad cases were escorted to the rear, including Roy's Captain, Sidney Eleveld.

As the regiment dug in and cared for its wounded, it collected the weapons they had captured as they overran German positions. The German Maxim guns were far superior to the unreliable French Hotchkiss gun and the noisy, inaccurate Chauchat automatic rifle.[5] It was those reliable, terrifying Maxim machine guns firing ten bullets per second, each bullet traveling 2,700 feet per second, that Roy and the Americans rushed, flanked, or crawled around and

---

5. Gansser, *History of the 126th*, 110–111.

disabled with only a rifle and bayonet.[6] Indeed, after the war, the commanding officer of the 126th blamed many of his men's deaths on the delay of properly equipping American soldiers on the front. For the moment, the Americans were grateful for every Maxim gun they captured in working condition. The second bit of news that cheered the exhausted 126th was that their artillery had finally caught up.

The next morning's advance started with a barrage. The artillery had been brought up to position four kilometers to the rear of the front line and opened up on German positions in the woods. For the first time, the 126th had proper artillery support and the thunderous roars of the guns behind instead of in front of them were greeted with cheers for themselves and insults to the Germans. Men who had lost friends in the last few days were pleased that the Germans could take their turn diving for cover. At 5:00 a.m., the cannons ceased and the regiment moved forward. Roy and Company K took the center of the first wave forward, trotting forward, eyes scanning back and forth for machine-gun nests. Their artillery had done their work well; the Germans only managed light resistance, and the 126th captured all of its objectives by early afternoon. At 2:00 p.m., they continued the advance beyond a plateau above the Ourcq River valley across a level field of grain. For a few hours, the long line of men trekked forward in the afternoon sun. Roy closed his eyes as he walked; it was like he was back in the Midwest, working on a farm. He managed a smile. The French countryside was beautiful.

The hungry, tired Americans kept going until the serene countryside was ripped apart by renewed German shelling. With a shout, Roy and Company K trotted forward to support the forward

---

6. Persice, *11th Month, 11th Day, 11th Hour*, 287.

scouts taking fire. The Germans were falling back to the next defensible line near the Vesle River, but it was an orderly retreat. The Germans were offering just enough resistance to allow their men and horse-drawn artillery to escape.

The advance continued. To support the thin American lines, the French sent cavalry equipped with carbines and long lances to look for the enemy and gather intelligence. This was the first and last time Roy would see the outdated cavalry along the front. Following the mounted scouts at a distance, the 126th advanced in a great line out of the woods and up and over the highest point of ground in the area. Opening up before Roy were fields of crops stretching to the right and left as far as the eye could see. The sun illuminated the landscape of gentle sloping hills, with patches of woods separated by deep valleys and gullies. All around, Roy could see lines of olive drab doughboys advancing line upon line along the whole front. In the distance, the Germans were in full retreat, burning war materials, streaking the sky with columns of smoke from giant fires. To the right, they could see German airplane hangars in flames, and directly in front, at a distance, a burning ammunition dump with black smoke and sporadic explosions. The Americans found it majestic, a mix of ancient and modern, picturesque yet deadly.[7]

The advance stopped at a high point about two kilometers south of their goal, the Vesle River. Seeing the goal and reaching it were two different things entirely. The Germans had dug in, and began to make life miserable for the advancing Americans, keeping the shells coming throughout the day and night. Adding to the misery, the rain came down in buckets, filling the fox holes and ditches. Since those ditches and fox holes were their only cover, the

---

7. Gansser, *History of the 126th*, 116–117.

Americans quickly became soaking wet and miserable. In these conditions, even the mud became an enemy. The heavy German shells pulverized the earth, and the heavy rain gave the shell holes the consistency of quick-sand. Some men slipped into the craters and drowned in the mud before help could come.

To make matters even worse, the American artillery was behind again. They would have no support from their heavy guns. The Germans also had complete air superiority, which meant they knew exactly where the 126th were digging in. The only recourse for the Americans was to somehow advance far enough and fast enough to get under the minimum range of the guns. Advance they did, charging through a downpour and driving the Germans from their strongholds on the south side of the river.

These small victories for the 126th came with a heavy cost. Barely had the 126th finished rudimentary defensive positions when the Germans let loose a deadly barrage of shells. They rained down so many gas shells that many of the Americans uniforms turned the greenish color of the gas. The Americans were forced back about 275 meters (300 yards) to some dugouts and caves. Refusing to give up, the Americans rested for a few hours and then advanced again. This time, the Germans waited too long to fire on the American advance. Led by Roy's Company K, the Americans trotted forward, keeping ahead of the shellfire until they reached the cover of the steep wooded slopes on the northeastern edge of the town. As Roy's Company K moved forward in a frontal assault, a well-timed flank attack from the 4th Division distracted the Germans. The defenders swung their artillery to meet the new attack, and Roy's company slipped through their defenses, taking the town and advancing to the river. Going further forward was impossible, though. The Vesle River was 7.6 meters (25 feet) wide and 1.8 meters (6 feet) deep at this point, and filled with strand after strand of barbed wire. The Americans now waited on their side of the river, taking whatever cover they could find. Their artillery caught up and began to open up on the Germans, which quieted some of the enemy fire. The 126th had reached their objective. The question was whether command would tell them once again to push forward.

At dark, Roy received word that they were to be relieved. His commanding officer, exhausted and worn down by the number of casualties, admitted, "It was like a message from heaven." They had been fighting non-stop for eight days, faced intense shelling, machine-gun fire, and hand-to-hand fighting. Before noon on the next day, August 7, they were replaced in the lines and carefully made their way back to a rest sector. It wasn't paradise, but it was far enough back that the shells could only be heard and not experienced firsthand.

Roy's part in the great Allied Offensive in the Second Battle of the Marne was over. He and the battered men of the 126th were looking forward to a bed and a warm meal.

Captain Gannser of the 126th related this poem that fit the mood of the frayed Yanks as they headed away from enemy lines:

AFTER THE BATTLE
The doughboy swung back from the fight,
The hard-fought battle won;
And in his eyes a shining light,
Out-gleamed the noonday sun;
Did he then boast about the fray
And tell each "why" and "how"?
The only thing I heard him say
Was, "Where the hell's the chow?"

CHAPTER 8

★ ★ ★ ★ ★

SHOCK TROOPER

*The 32nd Division was one of America's shock divisions,
it having been designated as such ever since it became a
combat division. While considerable glory may rightfully
be claimed by any organization selected to be shock troops,
such assignment usually carried with it the most severe
fighting which troops were called upon to do. To shock
troops fell the difficult task, every time the Huns became
obstinate and refused to budge from their stronghold, to
pry them loose from their positions and give them a fresh
start toward the Rhine, and this was by no means an easy
operation.*
—EMIL B. GANSSER, CAPTAIN,
126TH INFANTRY REGIMENT

*Over the top into the worst machine gun fire I ever saw . . .
VanDyke fell, Hoover fell, Edwards fell . . .*
—ROY'S DIARY, AUGUST 1918

─────────★ ★ ★ ★ ★─────────

Roy FOUND IT hard to credit survival to any skill on his part. The shells fell at random amid men on the fire-step, in the deep dugouts, or in No Man's Land as they advanced toward their objectives. Still, he had survived and hadn't run at the sound of the guns nor frozen when it was time to do his duty. In the midst of the worst of it, he fought for the soldiers on either side of him and tried to remember why the Americans had come to France in the first place.

Pershing was pleased with American efforts this far. American divisions had helped the French and British halt the final German advances toward Paris. The Americans had also been a key part to an ambitious counterattack that surprised the Germans with its ferocity and erased all that Germany had fought so desperately to gain in the spring.

The Germans now admitted that outright victory was impossible. The sheer number and quality of American soldiers daily arriving at the front destroyed all hope. The German Army had destroyed the Russians, trounced the Italians and Romanians, demoralized the French, and exhausted the British. But, the Americans had power that had just begun to be tapped and nowhere could the Germans draft, enlist, or conjure up adequate forces to counter the enthusiastic and nearly unlimited supply of American soldiers. At this point, it didn't matter if the Americans fought well or not. The Germans could not force them to surrender; their only hope was to hold out long enough for a favorable peace settlement.[1]

---

1. Keegan, 410–411.

The Yanks fought well, but Roy's regiment needed to catch their breath before they could continue to break through German lines. The first thing Roy noticed as they headed to their reserve station was who wasn't there. Out of the 3,300 men who had marched with Roy toward the German lines just a few weeks before, only 2,300 now traveled to the reserve area. Of his comrades from Grand Rapids, 122 had been killed, over 700 were wounded, and 10 were missing—either they were lost, blown to pieces, or drowned in the mud, nobody yet knew. As Roy walked into the Du Pelger Woods on August 7, his feet ached, his stomach growled, and he was crawling with lice.

Roy and the other 200 men of Company K made themselves as comfortable as possible amid the shell-torn wreckage of the reserve sector. Roy constructed a shelter out of a piece of corrugated sheet iron. Next, he washed off some of the mud and the grime from his body by standing in the open and pouring cold water over himself using a captured German helmet. Then, he shaved off his two week old beard. As he shaved, he watched a detachment of men head over to begin burying the dead Americans and Germans that still lay where they fell in the woods. The soldiers in the burial detail covered their mouths and noses with handkerchiefs, dug proper graves, and carefully lowered the dead soldiers into the ground. Each grave was marked with a little wooden cross and the dead soldier's identification tag. They buried the Germans with the same care but marked their graves by placing a German helmet on a stick at the head of the grave. That evening, the soldiers enjoyed hot meals, gathered in fireless groups, and talked of home or things they had seen and experienced thus far.

The first nights were quiet and restful, except for the flies. The corpses of dead men and horses had drawn them, and now that the corpses were buried, they concentrated their attention on the soldiers. Roy brushed them away from every mouthful of food he ate. Any piece of uncovered food was swarmed so that it appeared as a lump of coal, and no attempt to get rid of them succeeded. The men were too tired to complain. None of the flies were shooting at them or relaying their positions to the Germans, so they opened their new rations of cigarettes, ate their hot food, and attended church services in the company of buzzing insects.

Roy took some time to himself to read letters from home. Pearl had written to him—it was nearly a month old now—but he slowly read line after line. Mildred had written him; friends from Grand Rapids had also written him. Over the space of three days, thirty letters from home had reached him—notes from another world. Roy let his mind wander back to sunny, humid, Grand Rapids. His friends at home heard thunderstorms rather than artillery, dug up crops rather than trenches, and enjoyed watching girls in their summer clothes walking along the street window shopping rather than grimy, lice-ridden soldiers swatting at flies.

But, time in the reserve sector also gave the 126th time to sharpen their skills. Officers believed that the war for them had shifted from static trench warfare to a war of quick, brutal advances and exploiting weaknesses. The officers led the men through new formations and special instruction on how to operate captured German weapons. Roy learned how to work a Maxim Machine gun, fire a Boche rifle, and execute new open warfare tactics.

The time was profitable but short, for by the fourth day in the reserve sector, they were no longer alone and at peace. German planes circling overhead spotted the camp, and soon after taps, large German bombers began to drop on the 126th. Roy and his comrades ran over, grabbed their rifles and lay on their back in the open field. They aimed carefully at the bombers and squeezed off shot after shot. They had no noticeable effect, but it felt good to return fire.

Despite being occasionally harassed by German bombers, the 126th was rested and prepared to rejoin the effort to push the Germans back to the Hindenburg Line. On August 24 at 9:00 a.m, they moved out. All the letters would have added more weight to his already heavy pack, so Roy respectfully tossed them into the fire before he left the rest sector. Getting mentally ready for this trip to the front was more difficult. Last time they moved to the front, he didn't know what to expect. This time, he knew he faced shelling, machine-gun fire, and sporadic meals and rest. Nothing, however, could be done. Roy knew he was in France to stop German atrocities, push them out of France, and convince them to give up. His commanding officers had been speaking during their training sessions at the reserve sector about becoming "shock troopers." They would be a key part of the giant hammer that broke through the brittle German lines. The artillery would disorient the defenders; Roy and his fellow soldiers would follow close behind, slow and steady, mopping up the scattered resistance and securing the trenches. It sounded simple in the training sessions, but Roy had no illusions as he marched forward. The Germans were not going to give up without a fight.

As Roy and the 126th came out of the woods, they beheld the rest of their division moving slowly toward the front. As far as Roy could see, French camions[2] were lined up and creeping along, driven by Indo-Chinese chauffeurs from distant French colonies. It was a massive, slow-moving traffic jam. No one knew exactly where they were headed, although everyone speculated. Looking out the back of the truck as they moved along, Roy gazed at flattened

---

2. Motor trucks

villages and shell-torn fields littered with barbed wire and divided by trench works. The roads they traveled were pocked by shells and traversed poorly by the springless trucks for fifty-five kilometers until they reached the picturesque town of Croutoy, twenty kilometers due west of Soissons. The men quietly piled out of their trucks. Nothing moved in Croutoy. It was empty, quiet, and eerie. The vast majority of the townspeople had fled the approaching German troops during the spring offensives. After helping set up battalion headquarters, Roy's company moved to the valley on the northern edge of town and camped in the orchards.

Their orders arrived soon after they set up camp. They were to unite with the 10th French Army and join the Oise-Aisne Offensive. The French had already made some progress but couldn't break through a hillside stronghold. The Americans had already proven themselves as courageous fighters, and now the Army planned to use the shock troopers of the 126th as a blunt instrument.

Sunday, the men went to church services in the morning and wrote to their families. As the darkness settled on the camps, German planes flew overhead, dropping bombs, missing their targets but making sleep difficult. Roy awoke from a fitful sleep to a steady downpour of rain. It was too muddy for drills, so the men instead checked and rechecked equipment and ammunition. That evening, the men gathered around to hear their orders. Roy's commanding officer told the men that they were heading for the front. The courageous 126th cheered and whooped. After twenty days of rest, they were ready to get on with it. They were tired of the snipers and bombers who were constantly out of reach and longed to take out some of their frustration on the German strongholds.

After dark, the 126th assembled and hiked column after column down the narrow country roads. They carefully crossed the Aisne

River at Vic-sur-Aisne on pontoon bridges. The moon shone brightly and reflected in the water as the troops marched in silence, no lights and no cigarettes. As they entered the approximate range of German artillery, the Americans switched formation to single file with five paces between men. They passed through Tartiers at 7:00 a.m. and stopped at a ravine two kilometers northwest of the town. They had traveled twenty-six kilometers, much of it through the rain, carrying heavy packs. When they finally stopped, some men simply fell over, packs and all, and slept even through the artillery were nearby and flinging shells right over their heads. Not all of the 126th made it to Tartiers. Many of the regiment fell by the wayside on the long march. Tenaciously, Roy made the march, and he had enough energy left to write in his diary before he slept, *"(I) do not expect to go into first line or attack."* He had not been so wrong since he arrived in France.

As the men slept through the *krump* and the scream of the artillery duels, the officers carefully scouted the German lines. Satisfied, the officers woke the men at 4:00 p.m. for dinner. After eating, Roy cleaned his rifle and pistol and put an edge on his bayonet. The artillery had ceased firing, and the approaching dark masked their movements a little; but as the men prepared to move to their positions on the front, the moon emerged, shining brightly, revealing all, and making every movement dangerous.

Roy's 3rd Battalion was ordered up to the front line on the right side of the 2nd Battalion with the 1st in reserve. Roy's Company K was to take the front next to Company L. The two hundred men of Company K were ready, willing, and experienced enough to know that things could go terribly wrong in a frontal assault. Nonetheless, they followed orders and left their relatively safe camps to head toward the front. In single file, they marched through the moonlit dark of the early night: five paces between men, fifty paces between platoons out of the ravine, cutting across the fields to the road. The lead men stumbled into barbed wire. Quietly, they unstuck themselves, then backed up and took the long way around the field. They found a road and politely greeted their French guides who were waiting to take them to the front. They set up headquarters and Company K took their position behind the bank of a road. The men noted that the 353rd French Infantry seemed a little too happy to be relieved, hustling out of their positions and giving little helpful information to the doughboys.

By 3:00 a.m., Roy was in his position. He knew little—about as much as the rest of the regiment. What they did know was that they were on the Juvigny plateau, a high, open ground cut up by ravines. The 125th was on their left, the 63rd French Division beyond the 125th; on their right was the 59th French Division. To the extreme right was a hill that was the highest spot on this section of the front with a slope going down gently to the front. Beyond the front was the solidly-built village of Juvigny nestled in the bottom of a ravine. The Germans clung to the hill, the railroad, and the village of Juvigny. That stronghold was holding up the Allied advance all along the front. Pershing had sent the 32nd division, the 126th Regiment, Company K, and Roy Blanchard as shock troops to smash through those defenses so that the Americans could continue to drive the Germans out of France.

The quiet march gave the men time to think. The hill sloping off to their right would be a challenging obstacle. The Germans were dug in, and the Americans would have minimal cover as they advanced. If the French and American artillery didn't knock out most of the machine-gun nests, the slow-moving American advance would be an easy target. Roy had seen soldiers bodies riddled with machine-gun holes. He had personally fired a Maxim gun. The sound itself was terrifying, like a rattlesnake with lightning strike and formidable range. He had also seen the result of the anti-personnel field guns, men blown to pieces by shrapnel, the survivors missing limbs, crippled for life. He thought of his former bunkmate Lawrence Knittle—his nerves shot from the incessant shelling, no longer able to go over the top. But the men on both sides of him were comrades; live or die, they would do it together. The atrocities that the Germans had committed for the last four years were grievous. Helpless civilians lay at the bottom of the cold Northern Atlantic thanks to the German U-boat campaign. The whole world was mad, and someone had to put things right. Roy inspected his rifle and bayonet, made sure his helmet strap was tight, and checked his sidearm.

German artillery began at 5:00 a.m. and lasted a half hour. When the barrage lifted, Roy and Company K stepped up to the fire-step and waited. They were told that the French artillery would give them a fifteen minute barrage before they were to go over the top. The barrage didn't come. Either the French hadn't received the message, or their orders had been changed—impossible to tell at this hour. What was certain was that the German gunners would be at their positions, unmolested, and with a clear line of sight at the assault. Roy's commanding officer weighed the matter for fifteen minutes and then decided that they would have to do without the barrage. He blew his whistle, and Roy and Company K kicked a toehold in the loose earth, grabbed hold of the top of the temporary trench, and scrambled over the top. Light was showing on the horizon, and the Americans were in the open, some of the teenage soldiers living the last few minutes of their lives.

Perhaps the Germans were waiting for the customary introductory barrage as well. Roy and the Americans trotted the 150 yards of gradual slopes quietly enough to reach the line before the Germans realized that an attack was on. Groups of the Americans to Roy's right and left momentarily stopped and kneeled, taking aim with their rifles, ready to provide covering fire. The Germans had been caught unprepared, and the Americans quickly killed dozens, largely with bayonets or trench knives—bullets could kill their friends rather than foes too easily in the tight quarters of the trenches. Dozens of the Germans threw up their hands and yelled, "Kamerad!" Roy found that the trenches directly in front of him were completely abandoned. First thoughts of relief quickly shifted to fear. The Germans often yielded ground they had sighted in. Roy, waiting for orders, took a moment to rest, hands on his knees and panting from the 150-yard dash. He looked to his right to the hillside stronghold. With sudden, awful realization, he saw the hillside bristling with machine guns pointed directly down at the length of the trench. He watched the Germans open up gun after gun, the *rat-a-tat-tat* of the Maxim guns, bullets zipping by and thudding into the dirt as the gunner swept the trench from side to side. Vandyke fell on his right. Edwards fell on his left. Hoover fell. Out of his peripheral vision, Roy saw a support trench line running left, he pivoted to take to that ditch, desperate for cover. Death trap! Flank attack! German troops in a long line were running toward them. Roy stopped in his tracks. Men following him from Company K slammed into each other, yelling at each other to back up. Roy froze—the trench was full of dead and wounded. The machine-gun bullets were zipping overhead, putting holes in the trench wall and thudding into the bodies around him. He had to move. Roy scrambled from side to side, taking any cover he could find. Bullets again hit the fallen men in front of him. The next series of bullets knocked him off his feet. Pain burned in his shoulder. He looked down to see blood seeping through the hole in his drab olive jacket. Groaning, he now crawled, but it was too late—the Germans had them in their sights, and three men in front of him got hit. The man behind him fell. Two bullets hit his pack. The pack was too heavy to crawl with. Despite the sharp pain in his shoulder, Roy wiggled out of his pack and began to crawl over the dead and dying.

The German gunners switched their attention to another target, and Roy lay still for a moment, then carefully climbed out of the trench. Shooting at the machine guns would only draw fire at his wounded friends, and he doubted his aim at the moment anyway, with his left arm all but useless. He decided the best option was to crawl to the American lines 150 yards away. There, he could send help for his wounded friends. He couldn't crawl and hold his rifle, so he reluctantly left that behind too. Yard by yard, he crawled, stopping from time to time to rest and breathe. His shoulder stung, and he was losing blood. Men from the second wave came up out of the original American positions to help, and finally Roy made it back to the American trenches. Pointing toward the German lines, he told them that dozens of Company K were dead or dying in the trenches.

He was directed with other wounded Yanks to an aid station in a giant cave. The mouth of the cave was big enough to drive an ambulance into. On the cool ground in the cave, soldiers with various injuries were sitting or lying down. A medic inspected Roy's shoulder, quickly cleaned and bandaged the wound, and directed Roy to the ambulance station. Next, they loaded him on an ambulance, which made the best possible time to the second-aid station and then to a hospital.

Roy was not alone in the ambulance or the hospital. Two-thirds of Company K had been killed or wounded in the deadly German counter-attack.[3]

---

3. Gansser, *History of the 126th*, 139–141. Roy Blanchard diary.

The next morning, he woke up with searing pain in his shoulder. His comrades in Company K slowly woke with him. They all had the same story: elation at the initial success followed by the horror of being mowed down by German machine guns. To make it worse, once the Americans had taken out the German machine-gun nests on the hill, there had been heavy shelling of the Allied position. Casualties were high, and they had watched their friends die in front of them. News trickled in that Van Dyke had died in the German trenches. Hoover and Edwards had somehow survived.

The hospital was vast and cared for nearly three thousand men, most of whom were from his 32nd division. The news filtered in that the 32nd was continuing to push forward, despite the heavy casualties. Certainly, better communication and better artillery coverage would have saved lives. The Americans, like the European armies in 1914, were reckless. They moved too often in the open field and attacked in units too closely formed. Tactics aside, the Americans were in too great a number to be stopped by the thin, exhausted German ranks.

Roy's shoulder healed fast. The bullet had passed right through. The nurses checked him often to make sure he was free of infection and administered a painful tetanus shot to his abdomen. Roy looked around the hospital and felt fortunate. Most of the wounds were from shellfire, and the survivors had missing limbs or terrible concussions. Some were shaking and muttering; some had a faraway look in their eyes; others' mouths gaped open.

As Roy got better, the Army issued Blanchard a new uniform to replace his blood stained one, and he sketched the new blouse sleeves in his diary. A transfer order came next, and he moved across the river and became part of the permanent guard. On his first night of guard duty, he arrested four drunks. Later that week, he found the time to write his mother a letter. She wouldn't understand deadly shells falling like rain or rotting corpses littering No Man's Land. Not wanting her to worry, Roy kept the contents of the letter conversational and light-hearted.

Sept 19, 1918

Dear Mother:

Well here I am again and now I'm all healed up and passed both physical exams preliminary to going to a casual camp and then to the company. Am feeling fine and am on the "duty list" here doing little light shifts as Corporal of the Guard.

I certainly hope everyone at home is well and happy. There is no hope of me getting any mail until I reach the company but there ought to be a bunch of it there. And I haven't been paid for two months and if steamboats were 3 cents per dozen, I couldn't buy the echo of a whistle.

We can obtain a four hour leave to visit Angers if we care to, but I have only been down once. A fellow has to watch out what he is doing or get run in by M.P.s for going on restricted streets.

I was disgusted with the town on the start. On one street we heard a high voice of a woman singing on the third floor and Red (my chum) groaned and hollered "First Aid" (That is yelled on the battlefield when someone gets hit). The street cars runs within two feet of the curb and sounds like a "dog-in-the-ash-can."

The day I went to town I was crippled up with an awfully sore "tummy" as I got a "shot" in the abdomen the day before, as a prevention against lockjaw.

Gee, I hope they issue me a razor soon, because I hate to keep borrowing one.

I just bought a bunch of blades for my own razor, before going on the line the last time and then when I got wounded, I had to throw my pack away. I had two cans of Union Leader and two Bull Durham's, toilet articles, eating apparatus and a blanket, besides a can of Bully Beef and it went with the pack. The fellows often laugh here and say "I wonder where the little old bent, black mess kit is." Then we laugh. I got a nice new shiny one now. We are getting good grub and plenty. I eat so many peas I nearly roll out of bed nights and macaroni is very welcome on my plate even if they are slippery things to handle. We have nick names for every thing we eat. Corned beef is called either, "red horse," "monkey meat," "Bully beef," "corned willie," or "Canned Bill." Coffee is called "mud." Soup is called everything as—"slum," "slumgullion," "swill" or plain "chow."

Mother, I do hope that my army habits don't linger to embarrass me in civil life, but for the first month I'll hang a sign on myself as an excuse for my unsophisticated method of doing things in public.

I lost about 15 pounds since I came to the hospital, and weigh only 135 now but once I get started again, I'll let out my belt for a couple feet.

Listen, a nurse up in the Paris hospital asked the lad beside my bed where he was hit. He said in the front line. She said no, she didn't mean where on the field, but on his body. He blushed, grinned and said, "Once in the arm twice in the leg— and here he grew fire red and burst out with "Well if it had been you, you wouldn't have been hit." She looked at me and I said "Good night, nurse" and dove under the sheets. She said "Good night blondie."

Another fellow was slightly wounded where he [was] supposed to sit down and when he was making his bed, a nurse passed by and hit him a wallop. He jumped about six feet and landed on his serving tray and when she asked him why he jumped so, he just said "Because it hurt me!" She found out later about his inconvenient wound and smilingly apologized.

Well Mother, I have decided to settle down when I get home. Am sick of traveling and have seen enough of the globe to suit me.

I don't know if I have any money in the bank and I don't care, because if I haven't then I know it has some good at home, and if I have, don't tell me how much because I don't want to know until the right time.

I increased the allotment to $20 because I had a chance and besides I could easily get along on what I had left. I draw between 75 and 85 Francs every pay day and I don't gamble[4] and the only drink I care for is once in a while a cold beer a bottle of champagne (champagne is as common here as beer in the US) if I can get where there is a commissary I store up smoking and buy hot chocolate, cookies or maybe I lug back a can of jam, peaches or apricots. I like figs which are very plentiful and a lot of my money goes (this is when we are billeted in a populated town) to the kind old French woman who takes a half doz. eggs and makes an omelet and French fried spuds, not charging anything but the eggs.

You remember me writing from a little village where I had an M.P.s job, quite a while ago? It was called Percy La Grande, a town untouched by the hand of war and once lorded over by a certain Percy the Great. I often longed to go back to that village, because the population all turned out the afternoon we left and most of the women and children wept, for we had

---

4. Along with the cigarette habit, this came and went.

certainly had a stand in there. Most of the men were away in service, so we cleaned the streets of the town every other day and when off duty, we often helped the old men and women in the fields.[5]

Our M.Ps kept the two cafes quiet and keep strict street orderliness. Every night I took a little pail and brought milk from a milk seller and she never failed to be at home and invited me in to dinner two Sundays.

Will write soon again.

>*Your Loving Son*
>*Corp. Roy Blanchard*

If Roy had written to his mother about what the 126th was about to do, she would have indeed been worried. The Allies had been arguing about where the next great offensive should be launched and by which combination of forces. After long deliberation, General Pershing won the argument and launched a massive offensive, labeled Meuse-Argonne, using exclusively American forces.

The offensive started off well enough. When the American First Army attacked on September 12, it found the Germans in a state of retreat. But, while they advanced to the Argonne Forest and reached the defense lines that the Germans had been strengthening for years, the American army stalled. Many of the divisions that Pershing used were brand new to the front and ill prepared. At times, the whole offensive threatened to unravel. Despite sending 250,000 American soldiers against a German defense force of

5. Most men in the 32nd Division had very fond memories of the Alsace region. Joint War History Commissions of Michigan and Wisconsin, *The 32nd Division in the World War*, 46.

50,000 and employing 169 tanks led by a confident Colonel George Patton, the Americans were unable to reach their objectives. The terrain favored the German defenders, and the Americans were unable to effectively coordinate their attacks. Despite Pershing's threats and personal visits, the inexperienced American troops were unable to penetrate the stiff German defenses. To make matters worse, the Americans were unable to efficiently move their troops where they were needed. The confused troop movements resulted in massive traffic jams in the rear areas. By October 1, the entire Meuse-Argonne offensive had ground to a complete stop.

In the midst of all this, Roy was finally cleared to rejoin his regiment. Getting back wasn't easy. It took Roy nearly two weeks by train, camion, and foot to make his way through the chaos to his regiment. The reunion was happy; Roy and his comrades were thrilled to see each other still alive. After catching up with his friends, Roy gratefully opened the letters from home that had arrived since he was in the hospital.

As Roy looked around the regiment over pancakes the next morning, he saw many unfamiliar faces. The battle of Juvigny where Roy was injured had been costly for the 126th. The regiment was reduced to 35 officers and 1,750 men.[6] The effective fighting strength of Roy's company had reached as low as one-third its original number. While Roy was in the hospital, 1,100 replacements joined the regiment. Roy didn't have much time to get to know the new members of the 126th. The 32nd Division was packing up and on the move again; they were desperately needed at the front.

By October 1, 1918, the 32nd division including Roy and the 126th were in position in the sector between Verdun and Metz. They, along with the experienced 1st and 3rd Divisions, had

---

6. Gansser, *History of the 126th*, 157.

replaced the inexperienced divisions at the center of the American lines. As Roy and the 126th took their position, they looked out on craters, barbed wire, and ruined towns. It had been the setting for continued fighting during the last four years, including the massive Battle of Verdun. The Germans had extensive defenses set up in front of them, making the Americans' job straightforward. The 32nd Division had been given the task to punch a deep hole in German lines on either side of the Argonne Forest.

Punching a hole into German lines, however, was easier said than done. The Germans had perfect observation posts on the hills, a well-designed trench system, and perfectly positioned machine-gun nests. With every attempt the 126th made to advance, the Germans poured artillery on their positions. Day after day, Roy fought in the cold rain and thick mud. Before each advance, Roy thought of home, the men on both sides, and why they had come to France in the first place. The casualties for the 126th continued to escalate.

At the same time that Roy's 126th was fighting for every yard of territory outside the Argonne Forest, one of the most famous episodes of the war was happening inside. Many of the guns that were giving the Americans so much trouble were located deep inside the Argonne Forest. The guns, pouring down murderous fire on the slowly-advancing Americans, threatened to undo the progress they had made and even threatened to push them back. The 77th Division was assigned the task to silence the guns. Unfortunately, the large Argonne Forest was dense and prevented units from communicating well enough to work together. Each battalion ended up fighting its own little war. Because of the importance of their task, the men were ordered to hold any ground they took.

Most of the officers took that order with a grain of salt—everyone except Major Charles W. Whittlesey, commander of the 1st Battalion of the 308th Infantry. On October 2, Whittlesey's battalion set off with 670 men with orders to push forward to their objective on the road between Binarville to Apremont. Whittlesey's battalion found a gap in the German line and pushed through, reaching their objective before nightfall at a cost of ninety men. Early the next morning, they were discovered by the Germans and endured heavy mortar fire. Whittlesey sent a company of fifty men out to request help; only eighteen returned. Next, he sent out the first of his six carrier pigeons with a report. By the time headquarters received Whittlesey's second pigeon, the report was dire. His battalion had lost 222 men, 82 of them killed; and they were running low on bandages. Headquarters tried to send reinforcements and supplies but could not reach him. Headquarters, responding to his third pigeon, next shelled the forest where they believed the Germans to be. The fourth pigeon carried a message that they were being wiped out by friendly fire. Knowing the men were thirsty, hungry and fatigued, headquarters next sent in planes that dropped supplies. Regrettably, those landed on German-held positions. Despite all the hardship, Whittlesey's "Lost Battalion" held on, inspired by their injured, following a commander who refused to give up the ground he had gained.

On October 7, the German commander requested that he surrender. Although Whittlesey was down to less than 200 able men, he refused with a simple, "Go to Hell." Relying on coordinates relayed to them from American pilots, the Americans were able to push through the German lines and relieve Whittlesey's Battalion later that day. Only 194 men were able to walk out.[7] Whittlesey's efforts had not been in vain, for the Germans, distracted by the island of Americans, eventually fell to the men sent to rescue them.

---

7. Eisenhower, *Yanks*, 228–232.

One of the men sent with the 82nd as part of the relief operation was Tennessee sharpshooter, Alvin York. When his company's advance was stopped by a murderous barrage of machine-gun fire, he led sixteen men to knock it out. After nine of his men were killed by the machine-gun nest, the enraged York found adequate cover and shot twenty-eight Germans without missing a shot. The German major surrendered the rest, and York came back to his company with 132 German POWs.

While some Americans found glory and others found a muddy grave, the brutal routine continued for Roy. Without regard for casualties, the 32nd slogged forward with the assistance of both artillery and tanks. The Germans fought desperately for every yard of earth, sending shells, firing withering machine-gun blasts, and sending squadron after squadron of airplanes. The planes swooped down on the advancing Americans, strafing their ragged lines with machine guns, and bringing back information on troop positions to the waiting artillery. The Americans countered by setting up machine guns in strategic positions, taking aim at the daring German aviators. Next, the German artillery found the range and scattered the machine gunners, starting the process over again. Day after day, the Americans pressed forward. Preceded by rolling barrages, they took objectives and then dug in quickly as the Germans fired an endless hail of shells and bullets into their previously held positions. One innovation helping the Americans was the marvelous armored, machine-gun toting cars. The British had named them tanks.

Tanks, armored cars that used caterpillar tracks to traverse the rough terrain of No Man's Land, came into use in 1916. The British first used them in large numbers successfully at the battle of Cambrai in late 1917. The Americans, working closely with the French, used Renault tanks, light six-ton vehicles with a fully rotating turret and room for a commander and a driver. It was sixteen-feet-long and nearly six-feet-wide. It was armed with either a 37mm gun or the more typical 8mm Hotchkiss machine gun. As the 32nd Division moved forward, the tanks were used to clear a path for advancing infantry against machine-gun nests.[8] Unlike the vulnerable infantry, the drivers could advance over ground with little cover against machine gunners. The lightweight tanks had a top speed of four to five mph and gave opposing Germans a good excuse to surrender.

American Troops Ride on Tanks Going Toward the Front, Sept. 1918

Despite the help from the tanks and the experience gained from time on the front, the more the Americans advanced, the more difficult the task became. The last and strongest organized

8. http://www.firstworldwar.com/weaponry/tanks.htm, accessed July 31, 2015.

defensive position in this region lay before them—the Kriemhilde Stellung, the German's second defense line.

The first two attempts to break the line were unsuccessful. Roy's 3rd Battalion was chosen to be the attacking unit for this third attempt at breaking the Kriemhide Stellung. It didn't start well. At 5:30 a.m., the creeping barrage began. Roy expected the whistle to come soon after the creeping barrage started. It was important to follow the shelling as close as possible so that the Germans would just be getting to their positions when the Americans came storming into their trenches. But, something went wrong; by the time Roy heard the whistle, the barrage preceding the advance had already moved beyond the line of enemy trenches. As Company K made their way as quickly as possible through the barbed wire and pulverized mud, Companies I and L were beaten back with a furious hail of machine guns and rifle fire. Out of the corner of his eye, Roy saw the men fall and cry out. Increasing their speed and determination, Company K managed to make it through the enemy wire and onto the road beyond; but the Germans responded from enemy trenches on the bank above the road. Their expertly placed machine guns opened up from positions on the ridge. For a moment, it felt like Juvigny all over again. This time, Roy made it through the counter attack unscathed, but the advance was effectively halted. Company K dug in and waited for help. Responding to their requests, a small patrol from Company M moved up to clear the machine guns. From tree to tree, the Americans sprinted, taking cover in abandoned trenches or shell holes, creeping closer to the hostile nests. As the patrol drew enemy fire, a few brave soldiers crawled stealthily forward, flanked the machine-gun nest, shot three members of the nest, and captured the rest. The other Germans on the ridge, seeing one of their machine-gun nests fall, panicked and shot wildly at any movement. The Americans kept their cool, executed their assault training flawlessly, and eliminated or captured the remaining Germans.

The work wasn't done. After noting the casualties—ten percent of the attacking force—the 126th advanced again. They sent out scouts, determined weak points, and attacked again. They captured the city of Romagne and moved forward still. Pershing knew that if they let up, the Germans would only dig in better. This meant never-ending assaults. Roy wondered how much longer the 126th could continue the frenetic pace.

On October 15, the rolling barrage started at 7:00 a.m. Roy watched from the reserve positions as the 1st Battalion led and the 2nd supported, going forward only after the 1st and 2nd had secured the first line of trenches. Finding early success, all three waves advanced forward. By early evening, they were deep into German lines. When they stopped to dig in, the rain began to fall, and shortly thereafter came the first round of German shells. After the first rounds hit, Roy decided to take one of the large shell holes instead of digging in next to his platoon. The rain intensified again and with his back against the front of the shell hole, he watched the water level slowly rise. He considered finding a better place to hole up, but the Germans intervened before he could relocate. In the distance, he heard the *krump, krump* of heavy artillery. Next, he heard the familiar scream of the shells getting louder and louder. Pushing back against the front of the shell hole, he made himself small and covered his head with his hands as the shell exploded yards behind his position with an awful red blast and pulverized mud showering the hole. At the same time, the Germans in the distance let loose a salvo of machine-gun fire zipping overhead. Roy looked down at the water level again; it was slowly rising. The rain drops were now coming down in sheets, and he was soaked to the skin. He needed to find a better hole before he sank in the mud. After one of the large shells lit the surrounding landscape, he crawled with his rifle on top of his arms toward the last direction he had seen the rest of his company. Not far from the flooding shell hole, he heard a groan and followed the sound, sliding into another shell hole with a fellow Yank.

"Hit, bud?"

"Yes," came the reply.

Roy opened his comrade's jacket. Blood covered the young man's chest. He was shot through the lung. It looked bad. He looked his comrade in the eye but didn't know what to say. He bandaged the wound the best he could and told his new friend he was carrying him out. Carefully, he stood and started to pull the wounded man up. The wounded man let out a cry of pain, and the night split open, *rat-a-tat-tat.* Machine-gun bullets hit the top of the shell hole in a steady stream. Roy fell back against the side of the shell hole. They weren't going anywhere.

"I'm sorry," the young man apologized.

"Just hang on," Roy told him.

The young man said he was only seventeen, and his name was Jimmy. "I'm not going to make it," he said. He slowly opened his pack and brought out a few pictures of his family.

Roy agreed to write Jimmy's folks back in Montana and send his personal articles, scratching down his address in his diary. About midnight, the young man breathed his last, and Roy closed the young man's eyes so that they wouldn't stare up into the rain.

He began to get up again and try his luck at getting back to his company. In the distance again, like a thunder storm, he heard the all too familiar *krump, krump.* The shells burst all over. Roy got small, pushed his back into the muddy front of the shell hole, and prayed. In between shells, he saw signal flares. The Germans were looking for any sign of movement. For the next three hours,

Roy shivered in the mud and endured the intermittent shelling. Around 3:00 a.m., the shelling ceased. Roy whispered a goodbye to his fallen friend and slipped out of the shell hole, crawling to the rear. After dawn, shivering and emotionally spent, he finally located his company.

The cold, wet, tired 32nd kept fighting. Joined now by the reckless and determined 42nd , they put constant pressure on the Germans. The 42nd, spurred on by a brigadier commander named Douglas MacArthur, captured the key stronghold of Côte de Chatillon. Working on their right flank, the 32nd captured the intimidating Côte Dame Marie. The Germans could not recapture the heights; the Kreimhilde Stellung had been overrun.

The Germans had little reason to keep on fighting. The Americans had shown their willingness to fight on despite enduring heavy casualties. Germany's allies had all given up. The Bulgarians had opened negotiations with the French and British for an armistice on September 29. The British and their Arab allies were finishing off the Turks in Palestine. Austria sent Wilson a note asking to begin negotiations for an armistice in early October. Germany stood alone, tottering, but still fought on, hoping for a negotiated peace rather than unconditional surrender.[9]

As the diplomats discussed terms for Germany's surrender, Roy and the 126th pressed forward, alternating between intense fighting and mopping up the scattered resistance.

On October 19, the 89th division moved up in the line to replace the tired shock troopers of the 32nd Division and the 126th Regiment, ending the offensive for Roy. The aggressive tactics and stout German defense had resulted in over 6,000 casualties for the division. Roy was one of the 14,000 who had

---

9. Keegan, 413–417.

survived the offensive. They trudged to the rest area, line after line of muddy, tired men.

Once settled into the rest area, Roy pushed aside the gloom, exhaustion, and memories of fallen friends and wrote to Pearl.

Oct. 29, 1918

Dearest Sis:

The ebb of time is casting fortune my way, as I am altogether and feeling like a Jerry[10], ready to bust.

Have received enough mail lately to ruin any office and it made me as happy as a ringing telephone. Why I feel just like a fire alarm. Am glad everyone at home is well and if you are as happy as I am you will all go busted.

I'm not anywhere near the coast and am not on the front line but I will shill a half can of beans. I am near enough to have our apartments (a hole in the ground with a tin over it) shaken but a rumble and not protected from the boxcars that are dropped from bombing planes. Oh! Boy them bombs splash.

Yes, I've had a bath. Listen, this is good. Before I caught my bath I had enough cooties to cover the Brooklyn bridge, to stop Niagara Falls, to shame a monkey and the Pied Pipers rats were small beside my cooties. Then we got a gas bath, a soap rub and our clothes put thru something that had an intoxicated effect upon those miserable flee bitten, sleep losers. But alas, now I have them again and once more my nights are a continuous round of delirious imaginations of big animals screeching in my ears, chasing each other over my neck, fighting on my wish bone or playing stump the leader on my face.

---

10. German Shell

Stilwell was not killed but is sick in the hops. Dick Covert was killed in our last little mussuh.

You remember Drake? The little pal o-mine that went to the ball game with You, Anna and I at Cresten Park. He is alive and well and is also writing to someone.

Now Sis, don't wow wow about this doughboy, because he ain't taking any more chances than necessary and is confident that he can pull thru if these Germans ever see where we got it over on them.

I'm no gloom spreader and I'd like to knock old Last. Cornell for a row of comfort stations for decorating any room with his hard luck pills.

If you want the truth go to Jerry De Boaer (you know him) or Dick Zoet. If you want to wait until I get home, I can beat them birds all around in Shooting the bull.

Will give em all my best and write soon.

Tell Ma, she's the best ma-ma a going and my true idea of a soldiers mother, or a soldier in the second line.

Your Lover
Corp. Roy Blanchard[11]

The rest area turned out to be a miserable muddy mess, but anywhere away from shelling and charging machine-gun nests was paradise for Roy. The longer he stayed in the rest area, the less time he'd have to be at the front—which dramatically increased his chances of getting home alive.

---

11. Roy's letters have been kept in their original form. His spelling and slang are intact. Most of the meanings are clear, but some of the inside jokes or sayings may be understood only by a brother and sister.

★ ★ ★ ★ ★

11TH MONTH, 11TH DAY, 11TH HOUR

In one part of the line near Le Cateau a German machine gun was firing at the British troops in the opposite trench until the very last minute. At precisely eleven o'clock an officer stepped out of their position, stood up, lifted his helmet and bowed to the British troops. He then fell in all his men in the front of the trench and marched them off.
—BRITISH INFANTRYMAN, 11 NOVEMBER 1918

The old show is finis and the crowd is going home
—ROY BLANCHARD, DECEMBER 1918

Oh light your pipe up buddy,
And fasten on your pack,
The footing may be muddy
Along our forward trak.
But we should worry when we see
What we are going for:
We're marching into Germany—
We've won the blooming war.
—EMIL B. GANSSER, OF THE 126TH

★ ★ ★ ★ ★

THANKS TO THE YMCA, the worst possible place for the 126th to rest started off well. Not surprisingly, after the initial gifts of hot chocolate, cookies, and cigarettes were consumed, it all went downhill. The 32nd Division had been in line longer than any other advancing American division and was exhausted in every way possible. The location that the Army designated for their rest, Montfaucon Woods, had been part of the German front lines and the years of pounding by artillery had reduced it to splintered stumps, shell holes, and pulverized mud. The pup tents were the only shelter for the tired men, and there was precious little level ground in between the shell holes to pitch them. Roy set up in a shell hole covered by a thin sheet of tin that rattled every time a German bomber dropped anything remotely nearby. More privileged officers set up offices, radio stations, and headquarters in trucks, surviving dugouts, or shacks.

It rained.

Constantly.

Fires weren't allowed or desired since they attracted bombs from the German planes that flew overhead. No one got warm, and no one slept much amid the racket of flying planes and ineffectual anti-aircraft fire. The men did finally get cleaned up. Leave began with a trip to the ruins of Avocourt where the men were deloused, allowed to bathe, and given clean underwear. Roy felt like a new man and had enough time to see which of his friends made it through the last series of battles. One friend he thought was dead turned up alive.

Roy determined to survive long enough for the Germans to realize they were beaten.

Rest was short for the 126th. They were experienced troops, and they were needed in reserve as the Americans planned a general attack on the first day of November, 1918. Just after midnight, the Allies opened up a violent salvo, firing more than 1,700 artillery pieces in a continuous roar. The constant flashes illuminated a thirty-two kilometer (twenty mile) front for two hours. The rain of metal and fire was too much for the German defenders; after the front line divisions charged forward into the German lines, the Germans gave up or scattered.[1] Roy's 126th moved quickly to keep up with the moving front. Forward they marched: through villages, over rivers, and up heights. The only German counterattacks were from the bombers that harassed them after darkness.

The weather continued to worsen. Fall rains were frequent, the nights were cold, but the news drifting in kept Roy cheerful. They received word that the Kaiser had abdicated. The men gathered in groups as someone read aloud from the Paris editions of the Chicago Tribune and New York Herald, noting the progress of the Allied armies. The 126th could see it with their own eyes: the Germans were falling back all across the front. Word circulated that the Germans had sent emissaries to the Allied High Command.

But still the bombs dropped.

Still the high caliber shells dropped into the vicinity of the 126th.

Still the Germans fought rear guard actions, holding up the American advance with machine-gun fire.

The trench warfare was over, but the fighting was not. The Germans did not have the aid of concrete works or lines of trenches or wires. As the Americans moved forward, they could see evidence of abandoned trench efforts, but the Germans were moving back too quickly to fully dig in.

---

1. Ibid., 199–200.

The Allies, knowing that the German government and military morale were collapsing, kept pushing. Wilson wanted the war to end. He didn't want any unnecessary deaths among the brave Yanks that he had sent to France. Pershing took a longer view and disagreed. He believed that the best hope for a long peace was a thoroughly demoralized German army. Wilson wouldn't hear it and began to listen to German discussions of an armistice.

On November 10, the regiment moved forward again, passing through Haraumont to Breheville. That night, the ground froze, requiring some men to chip the frozen earth off their boots with shovels.

The next day broke like every other recent morning, with the boom of artillery and the splash of exploding shells spewing mud and dirt and shrapnel. The *rat-a-tat-tat* of the machine gun could be heard all along the front. The 126th had standing orders to relieve the 5th division at the front. At 9:00 a.m., the forenoon messages were received at Regimental Headquarters that an armistice had been signed. Hostilities would cease at 11:00 a.m. Rumors had been rampant for weeks, and they were not yet on German soil, so the message was regarded as a likely hoax. Still, they set their watches. At 10:30 a.m., the Germans began to shell the little village of Ecurely; one of the shells exploded near Regimental Sergeant Major Percy Baldwin, seriously wounding him. The Americans, enraged, returned fire until the German guns fell silent at 11:00 a.m. The 126th, still in disbelief about the armistice, didn't cheer.

Other regiments in Roy's 32nd division had assaulted several German positions on November 10 and suffered heavy casualties. Several of these regiments had orders on the morning of November 11 to assault German lines. As the minutes ticked toward 7:00 a.m., the men prepared to go over the top. At the stroke of seven, men got a toe hold on the side of the trenches and lunged over the top.

Runners shouted from behind. They stopped in their tracks as they heard, "Finis La Guerre!" The war was over.[2]

Roy's 126th didn't believe the news that the war was over until that evening. They were cooking a hot meal when they began to see German flares and rockets head skyward. Then they heard the German cheers. Still, the troops were cautious and slept with their weapons by their side. The morning of November 12 broke quietly, and the men smiled nervously at each other. The unfamiliar quiet made them uneasy. Like waiting for the next shoe to drop, soldiers waited for the bombardment to begin again, but the guns had ceased firing permanently.[3] Soldiers at the front lit fires simply to enjoy the light that had previously been denied them. They could walk around without cover and talk loudly—and after so many months of living in desperate combat, every bit of normality felt like vacation.

The war was indeed over.

The news slowly trickled in about the details. After the Austrian-Hungarian Empire officially surrendered on November 3, the German navy had refused a suicide mission and chose to mutiny instead. Popular uprisings followed throughout Germany and quickly brought down the Kaiser's government. The Kaiser himself fled to the Netherlands, and the German commanders had agreed to the Allies' terms.

The end of the war seemed as pointless and tragic as the war itself. Instead of laying down arms immediately, the Germans kept firing until the eleventh hour on November 11.[4] The Allies

---

2. Joint War History Commissions of Michigan and Wisconsin, *The 32nd Division in the World War*, 124.

3. Paul Fussell, *The Great War and Modern Memory* (London: Oxford, 1975), 68.

4. Canadian soldier Private George Lawrence Price was shot dead by a sniper on 11 November at 10:58 a.m.

too kept up assaults where valuable men were lost up to the last minute. For some of the soldiers, the ceasefire came too late. All their friends were dead.

For many in the American command, it came too early. The Allies were not on German land, and the army was still dangerous. Many believed that the Allies should have utterly destroyed Germany's ability to recover. Pershing himself had unsuccessfully argued with Wilson that they needed to completely humiliate the German army in order to keep this type of conflict from happening again.

The soldiers who had come of age during war didn't know what they were going to do next. Roy simply exhaled a long sigh. He had survived and would make it back home alive as one of the 4,355,000 that had been mobilized to stop the German menace sinking American ships without warning. He was one of the 204,000 who had been wounded in action in France. Somehow, he was not among the 116,516 who had lost their lives.

But, he was not entirely well. Weeks in the cold and wet added to the wounds and exposure to gas. Like thousands of other soldiers in France, he was likely suffering from Influenza, which had spread throughout the exhausted troops. Instead of going with the regiment to occupy Germany, he got on a train to Nantes, headed for a convalescent camp for those with non-life-threatening injuries.

Time in the convalescent camp was both comforting and troubling, especially for Roy. His stomach full, he now had time to reflect on what the war meant. The relief of not having to go over the top anymore was hard to contain. He thanked his fellow soldiers and "the goddess of war," for somehow surviving the chaos of the last several months.[5] Some of his bunkmates took the celebration to

---

5. Letter to Pearl, 1 December 1918.

a new level. The teenagers had discovered cognac and Benedictine and were drinking to excess, telling stories about French lingerie. Reflecting the Anti-Saloon League propaganda that drunks were flammable, he joked with Pearl that his bunk mates "stay(ed) away from the fire for fear of an alcoholic explosion."[6] He also steadfastly insisted that he wasn't chasing French women, comparing it to nervous hours on the front fearing gas attacks. In Roy's letters home, French women were "false alarms."

Mildred hinted in her letters that she imagined a proposal when Roy came back to Grand Rapids, but he told Pearl that it wasn't in the cards. He wasn't sure any longer that Mildred was the one for him, and he still didn't know how he could provide for a family. His bunkmates had discussed going into business together, and at least one seemed like a good plan. The army had taught him discipline and reinforced his instinct to work hard for the sake of others, but the pressure of making a living weighed on Roy. His father had bounced around from job to job—and family to family. The bitterness of his father leaving still hung on. He wondered how the man could just abandon the people who needed him and go his own way without caring whether they starved or became homeless. Roy thought too of how his commanding officers had faced the danger of battle with him. How they checked on him, cared for the wounded, and sometimes led the charge. It was time, Roy decided, to think of the future and forget the past.

Memories were already coming back to him in waves. Uniforms of fellow soldiers, rain falling, letters, glimpses of familiar landscape all brought it back. He couldn't get over his luck at surviving the war, and to Pearl he wrote,

---

6. Ibid.

11th Month, 11th Day, 11th Hour

Received a letter from a young French corporal who lives in gay Paris who has been mustered out. Was attached to the French in Alsace you know, last May and slept in the same dugout with him. He taught me French and I taught him English. Our dugout was blown to atoms one P.M. and as we happened to be out, we are still alive of course, but we lost every bit of equipment we had except a gas mask. That was one of the miracles that I never understood.

Another miracle was when two of us were lying under a piece of corrugated iron. My buddie went to see if we would eat that noon and while he was gone I crawled out and walked about three rods and opened my pack for a blanket. Just then a big Jerry came over and I flopped to the ground. It hit directly on the iron and blew everything to pieces. There was a hole about ten feet across and four feet deep, where we had been lying only five minutes before.[7]

Roy also heard back from Jimmy's family in Montana. They were grateful for the letter and news about Jimmy's last hours. They invited Roy to visit them, and he promised he would try.

As spring wore on, Roy grew tired of the company of soldiers. So many of them seemed content to get drunk, visit prostitutes, and get into trouble. Even the free entertainment at the YMCA became tedious. He joked about walking home and complained about the rain. He also told Pearl about his nightmares of drowning in mud.

Finally, the notice came that it was time to ship out. Roy took a train out of Nantes back to Brest. He looked out at the French countryside for the last time as he walked up the gangplank to the ship that would take him home. Close-up, the ship looked familiar.

---

7. Letter to Pearl, 4 March 1919.

After asking the sailors on the ship, he realized it was the troop transport that had originally taken him to France, refit as a hospital ship.[8]

After returning to Grand Rapids, Roy did his best to somehow put his life back together as a civilian. He and Mildred broke up soon after he returned. She was ready to start a family, but he wanted to wait until he figured out how to provide for one. The army tried to help in that regard by sponsoring his training to paint signs commercially. A local drug store hired him as their sign maker, but the pay was low and Roy moved on.

Looking for something more stable, he next took a job at a local manufacturing company, which worked out in unexpected ways. Since the relationship with Mildred hadn't worked out, Roy was actively looking for his soul-mate. The annual company picnic at Comstock Park turned out to be the opportunity he was waiting for. Like the other enterprising single men, Roy came prepared to the riverside picnic with a fancy canoe specially fitted with a crank-up phonograph. After lunch, in the custom of the day, the picnic emcee pointed out that fifteen men had brought their canoes, if any single ladies wanted to go for a ride. Young Lucile Heth was one of the dozens that strolled over to where the canoes were docked. Roy's quiet confidence and easy smile caught her eye, and she accepted his invitation to go for a ride. Roy took her on a leisurely sail on the Grand River and, in a sense, she never got out of the canoe. After a short courtship, they married on October 16, 1923. Roy worked hard to provide for her and their two children, Helen and Clark, painting signs and managing hardware stores.

---

8. Interview with Clark Blanchard, 20 November 2015.

Roy and Lucile, soon after their wedding.

During the Great Depression of the 1930s, Roy worked for the Marks Store in Grand Rapids. His work ethic convinced the owners to keep him on despite the desperate time. Roy repaid their trust by working seven days a week, twelve hours a day. His work ethic carried him through menial jobs and several failed business ventures with dishonest partners through the years. Roy's son Clark never heard him complain. Perhaps the lessons of war had taught him to laugh off the hard times. Again and again, he focused on the future and forgot the past. Having been through loneliness, poverty, and shellfire, he remained confident he could survive and simply chose to focus on the positive side of life—which included closing a negative chapter in his life.

Roy's father now lived close by the family. Tired of hanging on to his bitterness, Roy drove Clark over to meet his grandfather, John Blanchard. Thinking back on the event years later, Clark believed the purpose of the meeting was for Roy to show John that he had survived his betrayal and had become the father that John should have been.

Roy remained close to his sister Pearl, and even walked her down the aisle at her wedding years after Roy came back from France.

Roy walking his sister Pearl down the aisle
on her wedding day

Roy wasn't sentimental, and he never kept a diary again, but memories from the grand adventure in France came back to him from time to time with startling clarity. He told Clark about the dangerous planes that puttered overhead in long formations on the Western Front: "The Germans flew over us as we were in the rest areas behind the front, dropping small bombs on our positions," he said. "We lay flat on our backs on that cold autumn day, mad and helpless, firing in vain at them with our rifles. We didn't hit them."

Roy never drove. He explained to Clark when asked why he never got a driver's license that he was running across an open field with Company K in 1918 when the Germans opened up on them with machine guns and artillery. They all dove to the ground, and Roy's misfortune was to dive into a puddle with poison gas residue floating on the surface. Roy's sight in one eye would never recover. He didn't complain though. When a ride wasn't available, he just walked. "The government taught me to walk," he'd quip. Sometimes he'd sing funny songs to his children while they walked, echoing the songs he'd sung in his youth on the gravel roads in France.

He'd often speak quaint French phrases to his children and grandchildren. To his young granddaughter Amy, the tradition was to welcome her to his house and proceed over to the pantry where he kept the chocolates. The candies rustled as Roy shuffled to her seat and asked, "*Chocolat, mademoiselle?*"

Occasionally, on a Michigan summer's eve in the middle of a storm, the *krump, krump* of distant thunder would pull him back to his youth when he had heard thousands of active guns on the Western Front. With an intense whisper, he'd tell Clark, "Listen, Son—that sounds just like an artillery duel."

He'd also talk about the French, always with his trademark positivity. The beautiful country villages, adorable children that would see his uniform and beg for food and say, "*Merci!*" when he shared what he had.

Roy was a lifetime hunter. He taught his son to hunt with the same caliber of rifle he'd fired in France. But, when Clark came of age and expressed a desire to serve his country, Roy convinced him to join some other service besides the Army. When Clark chose the Navy and headed off to boot camp in 1954, Roy marked the day by giving up on his two-pack a day cigarette habit that had been solidified in his time on the Western Front.

Since Roy never moved away from Grand Rapids, the home of the 126th Infantry, he ran into his fellow guardsmen from time to time. Near the end of his life, he and one his fellow guardsmen that lived down the street would get together once in a while and reminisce about old times. After a few of those visits, the nightmares returned. There he was again, Corporal of the Guard on the Western Front. Scratchy wool uniform on, steel helmet fastened and tilted forward, the night lit by flares and the flash of artillery. The Germans were coming in waves toward the American trenches. Summoning his courage, Roy stepped up to the fire-step and leveled his Springfield rifle. But before he could pull the trigger, the barrel of the rifle wilted, like a week-old flower plucked from the ground.

Other nightmares were of running for cover in the shelled wasteland of the Western Front. The explosions and blinding flash of artillery all around him, slipping into a shell-hole filled with water, he began to sink with water and mud up to his knees, his waist, his neck, his chin. He awoke in a cold sweat, unable to shake the vivid images. He reluctantly told his friend that the visits would have to stop; the fond memories of the grand adventure had become a curse. As a teen, he had joined up to escape the monotony of an ordinary life. Now, his remarkable time in France needed to be put out of his mind and forgotten.

He poured his last years into helping mentally disabled youth learn a trade in Grand Rapids. A relative had started a school in the neighborhood and he volunteered with children that others had given up on. He found great joy teaching the teens life skills for employment and training them how to sight read bus signs so they could get from place to place. Step by step he taught them how to cope with challenges, help each other, go through their check points, and face their obstacles with courage. Thanks to Roy, the disabled youth had freedom to get from place to place, achieve independence, and contribute to society at last.

Roy's wife Lucile died in July, 1985. Alone again, Roy lost interest in life, and his health quickly deteriorated. On a cold November night in 1985, he called Clark, complaining about chest pain. Clark drove over and sped him to the hospital. As Clark accelerated faster and faster, Roy looked over and with concern commented, "You're running all the red lights."

"Yes, Dad, you are important!" Clark replied.

Roy smiled. The last time he was in mortal danger, in the trenches of far-away France, he had to drag himself to an aid station.

Roy died in November of 1985, nearly seventy years after his time in France. Before he passed away, he requested a simple family service at the family's congregational church instead of a formal soldier's service. After all, his time as an American soldier had long been over. His real adventure in life had been loving Lucile and raising Helen and Clark. Roy had bravely done his duty in World War I. He had held the line, braved the shelling, and gone over the top when the whistle blew. But more importantly, he had courageously broken the cycle of abuse and abandonment passed down to him by his father. He'd sheltered and provided for his family and cared for the helpless in his community. He had soldiered on, and that was all that mattered.

EPILOGUE

★ ★ ★ ★ ★

THE LAST CASUALTY

*All the nations that have power that can be mobilized are
going to be members of this League, including the United
States. And what do they unite for? They enter into a
solemn promise to one another that they will never use
their power against one another for aggression; that they
never will impair the territorial integrity of a neighbor; that
they never will interfere with the political independence of
a neighbor; that they will abide by the principle that great
populations are entitled to determine their own destiny and
that they will not interfere with that destiny; and
that no matter what differences arise amongst them
they will never resort to war . . .*
—PRESIDENT WOODROW WILSON, 1919

★ ★ ★ ★ ★

As Roy rode a railroad car toward a hospital near Nantes in November 1918, those in his regiment healthy enough to march traveled in the opposite direction. Villagers heard them singing before they saw them: "It's a long way to Tipperary, It's a long way to go. It's a long way to Tipperary, To the sweetest girl I know." The Yanks still sang as they marched, swinging arms, clad in khaki, their faces full of relief and the unshakable confidence of youth.

The villagers came out as one to see the "Americaine Soldaten." marching toward the Rhine. The villagers cheered, waved, and decorated their homes with their homemade red, white, and blue American flags. Marching toward Germany, the 126th passed airfields and manufacturing centers. In the distance, they saw the dust kicked up by the retreating Germans. The tension of war was gone. The men soaked in the new sights and sounds and smiled at the cheering villagers. This was what they signed up for—a victory tour.

By November 20, they entered Belgium, briefly crossed Luxemburg, and then returned back into Belgium. The occupants hung banners, "Hearty Welcome to Our Deliverers," lit fireworks, invited the soldiers to dances, and clapped as dignitaries gave speeches of thanks to the American troops. As the 126th entered the city of Echternach on the boundary between Belgium and Germany, they found the mayor and members of the city council in full dress suits waiting to receive them. The population lined the streets, and after the mayor had welcomed them, the town band, gendarmes, firemen, and boy scouts escorted the soldiers through town amid shouts and flowers from the townspeople. Amid the feasting and celebrating, commanding officers read a message aloud to the men from General Pershing. He asked them to behave "not as despoilers or oppressors, but simply as the instruments of a strong, free government, whose purposes toward the people of Germany are beneficent." The 126th spent the winter and following spring in Germany, drilling and resting until the first of May 1919, when the Army finally decided that it was time to send them back home to Grand Rapids.

With relief, the 126th loaded onto trains and took a slow, three-day ride to France. In Brest, the men took showers, received medical examinations, put on clean clothes, and waited for the English ship *Valacia* to arrive. Boarding on May 9, they went across the gangway and were directed to their berth. The voyage home went without incident, and the men were mustered out May 22, 1919. Their part in the long, brutal, costly venture was over. The Germans had been stopped, pushed back, and dismantled. The vexing question, however, still remained: could the politicians secure the peace?

American President Woodrow Wilson arrived in Paris in December 1918 to do just that. His words from the declaration of war in April of 1917 haunted him:

> It is a fearful thing to lead this great peaceful people into war, into the most terrible and disastrous of all wars . . . . But the right is more precious than peace, and we shall fight . . . for democracy, . . . for the rights and liberties of small nations, for a universal dominion of right by such a concert of free peoples as shall bring peace and safety to all nations . . . . God helping her, she can do no other.[1]

---

1. Quoted in Gene Smith, *When the Cheering Stopped: The Last Years of Woodrow Wilson* (New York: William Morrow and Company, 1964), 33–34.

Men had applauded wildly that day. How strange, Wilson thought, to applaud sending young men to their deaths.[2] And send them to their deaths they had. Over a hundred thousand young American men had perished in their attempt to remake the world. Wilson wondered if indeed the world could be remade. The task was daunting. The war had disrupted everything. Nations were starving, a flu epidemic raged, and governments across the continent were in various stages of collapse.[3] Even the most optimistic of men doubted a new order could be constructed out of the chaos. Wilson admitted to a friend,

> It is to America that the whole world turns to-day, not only with its wrongs, but with its hopes and grievances. The hungry expect us to feed them, the roofless look to us for shelter, the sick of heart and body depend on us for cure. All of these expectations have in them the quality of terrible urgency. There must be no delay. It has been so always. People will endure their tyrants for years, but they tear their deliverers to pieces if a millennium is not created immediately. Yet you know, and I know, that these ancient wrongs, these present unhappinesses [sic], are not to be remedied in a day or with a wave of the hand. What I seem to see—with all my heart I hope that I am wrong—is a tragedy of disappointment.[4]

The crowds cheered his arrival. School girls tossed flower petals on the road before him. Wilson smiled and tipped his hat

---

2. Ibid.

3. Herbert Hoover, *The Ordeal of Woodrow Wilson* (Washington: Woodrow Wilson Center Press, 1992), 70.

4. George Creel, *The War the World and Wilson* (New York: Harper and Brothers, 1920), 163.

to the cheering throngs in England and France. Never before had the Europeans been visited by an American President in office. Wilson hoped they saw their ascendance as a sign of peace and new hope. But, if the people of the world wanted peace and a new order, it certainly wasn't reflected in the leaders they sent to Versailles. Wilson's hopes, built on fourteen points that would assure the continuity of peace, ran up against the nationalist aspirations of Japan, Italy, Britain, and France. Wilson asked for open diplomacy, freedom of navigation upon the seas, free trade, minimal armaments, popular sovereignty, impartial settlement of thorny territorial issues in Europe, and the creation of a League of Nations that would be in place to solve problems that would normally lead to war. Wilson wore himself ragged trying to convince the Europeans that his ideals could be implemented.

After six months of bitter negotiations and devastating compromises, the Allied powers of Britain, France, and the United States presented Germany with the Treaty of Versailles. The treaty outlined serious conditions: Germany and its allies would accept full responsibilities for the war. Germany would give up all its overseas colonies. Alsace and Lorraine and the Polish-speaking areas of Germany were surrendered. Germany's army could from this day forward be no larger than 100,000 men. The German navy was drastically reduced. They were forbidden from having submarines, tanks, artillery, poison gas, or airplanes. The German Rhineland was to be demobilized and open to inspection by the Allies. The military high command was to be dismantled and leaders subject to trial for war crimes. Finally, the Germans were liable for whatever war indemnity that the Allies decided.[5]

---

5. $33 billion was finally agreed to in 1921.

The Germans had no ability to negotiate. Incensed and feeling betrayed, they signed the treaty.

The treaty didn't please the Allies either. France wanted Germany's ability to ever threaten its neighbors again to be dealt with decisively. Britain wanted Germany to be punished, but believed a healthy Germany to be a key to Europe's economy. Wilson wanted the treaty to be reasonable and based on justice rather than revenge. The treaty turned out to be a dreadful compromise that fulfilled none of those desires.

Wilson feared that any treaty that solely blamed Germany for the war was so demonstrably false that it would cause the next generation of Germans to rise up to take revenge. Obviously, the victorious Europeans were in no mood for introspection and insisted that Germany take the full blame for the conflict. Wilson's last hope for the Treaty of Versailles was the part of the Treaty that created a "League of Nations" which would provide a forum for fixing the treaty. Surely, Wilson thought, after a few years of peace and rational thought, leaders of Europe and America would come to their senses and change the treaty through the channels established by the League of Nations. The League would also provide a means to prevent future wars from taking place. If the US ratified the treaty, and provided leadership in the League, the Great War would truly be the war to end all wars.

So Wilson hoped.

But it was not to be.

The League of Nations, essential to the enforcement of the peace that had been purchased by so great a price by men like Roy, was in fact completely unacceptable to the United States.

The first warning signs came after US papers published details of the peace settlement and pointed out how the treaty seemed completely contrary to Wilson's fourteen points. Many Americans, disappointed with the punitive scope of the peace treaty, saw it as another case of the victor punishing the vanquished. Arguing intensely, Wilson admitted that the peace treaty was flawed but insisted that the League would serve as an instrument to right the wrongs in the treaty.[6]

The second ominous sign came when Wilson went before the Senate in July of 1919. Two of the senators even refused to stand while he entered. Ragged and worn, Wilson asked the Senate to ratify the treaty. The Republicans, however, controlled Congress. They believed the League would interfere with US national sovereignty and "entangle" the US in alliances.[7] Most objectionable to the opposition was article ten which stated,

> The Members of the League undertake to respect and preserve as against external aggression the territorial integrity and existing political independence of all Members of the League. In case of any such aggression or in case of any threat of danger of such aggression the council shall advise upon the means by which this obligation shall be fulfilled.[8]

Led by Henry Cabot Lodge, the Republicans asked that article ten be amended. Wilson refused to compromise on this article. He had already made numerous compromises concerning the rights of nations to withdraw from the League, exclusion of

---

6. Arthur S. Link, *Woodrow Wilson: Revolution, War, and Peace*, 102.

7. Henry Cabot Lodge, Senate Speech February 28, 1919, *The League of Nation* (Cambridge, The University Press, 1919), 22-25. Lodge and other Republicans believed entering the League of Nations would violate George Washington's principle against entering into entangling alliances with European countries.

8. Gary B. Ostrower, *The League of Nations: From 1919 to 1929* (New York: Avery, 1996), 21.

domestic issues from the League's jurisdiction, and clarification in the Covenant that it remained Congress's authority to declare war.[9] He knew further compromise would make the League of Nations powerless, unable to secure the peace or prevent future wars.

Wilson, facing the real possibility that the peace treaty and the League might go down in defeat, decided to take his case directly to the people. Noting Wilson's exhaustion, his family and doctor strongly advised against the tour, but he told his advisors that it was a matter of duty and that he could not put his personal safety and health in front of that.[10]

The tour began with disappointing attendance, but it gradually built in numbers and enthusiasm as Wilson made his way west. He gave speeches in Columbus, St. Louis, Kansas City, Des Moines, Omaha, St. Paul, Minneapolis, Bismarck, Billings, Helena, Coeur d'Alene, Spokane, Tacoma, Seattle, and Portland. As the crowds grew, his weariness intensified and forced him to make his speeches shorter and less frequently than scheduled. His train headed south to San Francisco, San Diego, Los Angeles, and then back east to Reno, Salt Lake City, Cheyenne, Denver, and finally to Pueblo Colorado. Although his voice would sometimes falter, he clearly articulated his arguments, and reminded the audience why he had sent soldiers like Roy Blanchard to war:

> You know how we regard the men who fought the Civil War. They did the greatest thing that was to be done in

---

9. August Hecksher, *Woodrow Wilson*, 588–589.

10. Gene Smith, *When the Cheering Stopped: The Last Years of Woodrow Wilson* (New York: William Morrow and Company, 1964), 58.

their day. And now, these boys here, [indicating soldiers] and others like them, have done the greatest thing that was possible to do in our day. As their fathers saved the Union, they saved the world. And we sit and debate whether we will keep true and finish the job or not . . . . Nothing less than that hangs in the balance. I am ready to fight from now until all the fight has been taken out of me by death to redeem the faith and promise of your action.[11]

He stumbled onto the stage in Pueblo, Colorado and a secret service man steadied him before he continued onto the podium. At the beginning of the speech, he stopped in the middle of sentences and seemed to repeat himself, often pausing for moments as he tried to collect his thoughts. Secret Service men behind him readied themselves to catch Wilson as he tottered, but Wilson managed to regain his strength and finish his speech. In this speech, the last of his presidency, Wilson spoke of the men who had fought for the US in the war:

And, if we did not see this thing through, if we fulfilled the dearest present wish of Germany and now dissociated ourselves from those whom we fought in the war, would not something of the halo go away from the gun over the mantelpiece, or the sword? Would not the old uniform lose something of its significance? These men were crusaders. They were not going forth to prove the might of the United States. They were going forth to prove the might of justice and right. And all the world accepted them as crusaders, and their transcendent achievement has made all the world believe in America as it believes in no other nation

11. Arthur Link, Editor, *The Papers of Woodrow Wilson*, 63: 234.

organized in the modern world. There seems to me to stand between us and the rejection or qualification of this treaty the serried ranks of those boys in khaki.[12]

Wilson barely made it off the stage following his speech. Stumbling back to his train car, barely able to walk without assistance, Wilson had to admit defeat. With tears in his eyes, he told his secretary, Joseph Tumulty, "The Doctor is right. I am not in condition to go on. I have never been in a condition like this, and I just feel as if I am going to pieces."[13] Tumulty subsequently canceled the remaining events and the train sped Wilson back to Washington, D.C.

The long series of decisions that Wilson had made intensified his grief on this occasion. Wilson personally despised war and had agonized for years over the decision whether or not to go to war against Germany. When the time came that war seemed inevitable, he soothed his own troubled conscience by telling himself and the world that they fought to end all wars, that they fought for all mankind, and that they fought for everlasting peace. The compromises that were made in the peace treaty were painful and potentially disastrous, but he believed all could be rectified by a strong League of Nations. As his speaking tour proceeded, he met parents of slain soldiers who told him of their loss mitigated only by the thought that their sons had died to bring peace to all. He promised those parents and he promised his supporters that the American soldiers had not died in vain. Wilson could not bear the thought of what failure would mean.

---

12. Ibid., 63: 512.

13. Ibid., 63: 519.

Days later, he suffered a series of strokes and became a near invalid for the rest of his term. The possibilities of peace according to Wilson's design would also fall victim to his uncompleted tour. The Senate refused to ratify the Treaty of Versailles or join the League of Nations. The public's rejection of Wilson's program for peace seemed complete as the Democratic ticket that supported the League of Nations went down to defeat in a landslide in the presidential election of 1920.

Wilson died in February of 1924. Without the United States and strong leadership, the League of Nations was unable to stop the aggression of Germany, Italy, and Japan in the 1930s.

The job of finishing the conflict begun in 1914 fell to the next generation. As Wilson had feared, angry Germans rose up looking for scapegoats for their ruined country. The discontents looked to a bitter World War I veteran, Corporal Adolf Hitler, for leadership. Hitler successfully blamed German troubles on the unjust ending of World War I and launched a brutal war of aggression that quickly overwhelmed France and nearly brought Russia and England to their knees.

As in 1918, American soldiers came to the rescue and bravely marched across the continent of Europe. The wisecracking G.I.s in 1944–1945 often fought over the same land where Roy Blanchard and the Yanks fought in 1918. The soldiers' tanks had better armor, their planes were faster, and the bombs more devastating, but the same sacrifice and determination were required.

The worldwide conflict of World War II was so compelling and the G.I.'s efforts were so consequential that they almost completely overshadowed the courage and sacrifice of the soldiers of World War I. Now, when Americans think of World War, they think of Pearl Harbor, D-Day, the Battle of the Bulge, and the dawn of the nuclear age over Hiroshima. Forgotten are the Yanks, teenage soldiers like Roy Blanchard, who sang while they marched, endured horrific shelling, and went over the top into the teeth of machine-gun nests on the Western Front in 1918.

Their story of courage deserves to be told.

ACKNOWLEDGMENTS

I AM INDEBTED TO many for this project's completion.

Thank you to my family for your support. First of all to Kathryn Dean, who supported me tirelessly on the 16-year journey to take this from idea stage to completion. To Nathan, Carolyn, Alaina, and Lizzie—thank you for understanding all those hours when your father couldn't be disturbed. Thank you to my parents Dr. Bill Dean and Marcia Dean who gave me a love for history and showed me how important it is to finish what I begin. Also, Dr. Jack Simons for offering valuable help, reading the manuscript, and offering helpful research suggestions. Thank you also to Martin Simons Esq. for reading the manuscript and providing helpful comments and suggestions.

Thank you to my friends, mentors, and colleagues at Washington State University. Especially Dr. Noriko Kawamura for her excellent help with the original project and Dr. Jeff Johnson for his support and encouragement.

Thank you to my friends in Michigan. Ted and Ruth Passineau for hosting me on my initial trip, and for introducing me to Amy Blanchard Bowden. I owe much to Amy Blanchard Bowden and Clark Blanchard, as well as the rest of the Blanchard family for sharing your priceless mementos and memories with me. Without you none of this would have been possible.

Thank you to those on the Seattle eastside who have helped support the project in various ways: Kevin Mather for your generous support and encouragement, and Chris Widener for helping me understand the book industry.

Thank you to the Library staff of Michigan State University, Wayne McElreavy, President of the Claremont NH Historical Society, and Google for digitizing obscure books and putting them online for anyone to read.

Thank you also to the capable staff at Lucid Books: Casey Cease, Sammantha Lengl, Laurie Waller. And to Laura Allnutt for her superb editing help.

CPSIA information can be obtained
at www.ICGtesting.com
Printed in the USA
FFOW04n1248130218
45088148-45483FF